M000280802

LUNCH with
the WILD
FRONTIERS

For Mum, Dad, Michele,
Kle, Scout, and Piper.

Lunch With The Wild Frontiers
A History Of Britpop And Excess In 13½ Chapters
Phill Savidge

A Jawbone book
First edition 2019
Published in the UK and the USA by
Jawbone Press
Office G1
141–157 Acre Lane
London SW2 5UA
England
www.jawbonepress.com

ISBN 978-1-911036-49-4

Volume copyright © 2019 Outline Press Ltd. Text copyright ©
Phill Savidge. All rights reserved. No part of this book covered
by the copyrights hereon may be reproduced or copied in any
manner whatsoever without written permission, except in the
case of brief quotations embodied in articles or reviews where
the source should be made clear. For more information contact
the publishers.

Jacket design by Paul Palmer-Edwards,
www.paulpalmer-edwards.com

Printed in the Czech Republic by PBtisk

1 2 3 4 5 23 22 21 20 19

CONTENTS

MUSIC PR

A GLOSSARY OF TERMS

Critically acclaimed	Highly unlikely to sell any records.
World-renowned	We've heard of them. No one likes them.
Multi-platinum	They've sold a fuck load of records, so that must mean some of your readers like them.
Grammy-nominated	They haven't won anything.
Pop Icon	*Artiste* beloved of those with diminished IQ.
Genre-defying	They don't know what they sound like, and we haven't got a fucking clue either.
Powerhouse chanteuse	Really shouts, not a chance of hitting the right notes. Oh, and she's a lady.
Avant-garde	Unlistenable.
Stadium-sized swagger	Yet to fill out the Dublin Castle.
Epic indie	They've got an FX pedal.
Intimate and laid back	You may be tempted to nap.
Legendary	Really old. Ask your mum and dad.
Enigmatic	Pretentious. Largely irrelevant.
Addictive	Chorus so obvious you could stick a fork in it.
Pioneering	Not famous.

THE GOOD OLD DAYS

Before it became a corporate behemoth, music public relations was one of the most entertaining ways to spend your working day. You could go out for lunch on a Monday and come back on a Thursday, and your office co-workers would applaud your indifference.

When you finally turned up, you could invent stories and then have the satisfaction of seeing them laid out in print the following day. You would have running jokes: when holding a meeting in your back room, you would run through your list of acts and then say, 'Right. Jesus & Mary Chain? Any feedback?' and the rest of the office would laugh along with the absurdity of it all.

Way back in the distant past, I represented a band called The 25th May. This terribly agitated, funk-punk collective—I suppose you'd call them agit-pop—were named after Argentina's May Revolution Day and used to pride themselves on causing as much trouble as possible (without actually breaking sweat), presumably as a diversionary tactic, to distract people from listening to their music. They were ridiculously, almost comically, left wing, and their manager used to call me every Monday morning to map out what stories we'd be making up that week. This usually involved pretending that there'd been some kind of riot at one of their gigs. I'd ring *Melody Maker*—always an easier touch than the *New Musical Express*—and suggest there'd been reports of fighting at the band's last show in Newcastle; the *Melody Maker* would ask me for a number for the promoter, and I'd patch them through to a friend of the manager who happened to live in Newcastle; after one conversation with the outraged 'promoter'—*Divvin' gan'n reet bad things, man, but it were oot of control*—they had a story. It went like clockwork.

CHAPTER 1

I HAVEN'T GOT TIME FOR EXPERIMENTS

"When I was ten years old, my mother stayed up all night making me a silver sequinned suit so that I could go to the school fancy-dress party as Gary Glitter."

When I was ten years old, my mother stayed up all night making me a silver sequinned suit so that I could go to the school fancy-dress party as Gary Glitter. I borrowed my sister's white platform boots and giant necklace and kidded myself I looked exactly like him. Glitter was currently enjoying success with his second no.1 record, 'I Love You Love Me Love', a song that would go on to be 1973's biggest-selling single.

Events went extremely well, and at the fancy-dress contest I was shortlisted into a group of three finalists. Next to me on the podium stood Robin Hood and Little Bo Peep, but when the headmistress smiled over at me, before climbing up on the podium, I knew my time had come.

'Ladies and gentlemen, boys and girls,' she announced triumphantly. 'And the winner is ... *Liberace*!'

Everyone—including my mother—clapped, and I stepped to the front to accept the applause. I glanced around the room at all the friendly faces and thought, *How could you not know who Gary Glitter is? He's no.1, for God's sake!* I still kept the sweets and the certificate, but I felt nothing but pity for those uninitiated in the finer delights of the pop charts.

Aside from *The Liberace Incident* (as it was always referred to by mother), it is important to point out that my school days were not particularly unhappy: I attended a prep school called Greenholme in Nottingham (which I only found interesting as the father of a child in my class, Tom Baker, was the incumbent *Dr Who*), and then, at the age of eleven, moved to Nottingham High School. At the age of sixteen, I was sent to Sherborne School in Dorset—my parents were in the process of relocating nearer my mother's birthplace—where I boarded for two years. This was not as easy as it sounds, as I had never actually spent a single night away from my mother and father, and the prospect of two years away from them filled me with dread.

It was an all-boys school, which was bad enough in itself, but perhaps the worst thing about it was the worst thing about any boys school: everyone was trying to be as macho as possible. In my first week, I tried to compete by drinking a bottle of whisky in a single sitting, but this only resulted in me being sent to the local hospital to have my stomach pumped. The following week, when I'd finally summoned up the courage to sit next to a group of boys at dinner, one of them asked if I played rugby.

'No,' I said. 'I play football.'

'That's a pity,' he said, ''cos I was looking forward to kicking your head in.'

The comment stayed with me throughout my first term. Whenever I found myself forced to play rugby, I made sure I could play on the wing, thus ensuring I'd avoid being squashed in the scrum. Sometimes, when I was unlucky enough for the ball to be thrown to me, I would run away as fast as possible and hope that I was running in the right direction. It's extraordinary to think that on several occasions I managed to get to the try line and plonk the odd-shaped thing down before anyone could pummel me to death.

Sherborne School was beyond parody. As far as I could gather, no pupil had ever met anyone born north of the Watford Gap, and I was immediately nicknamed *Butty*, since all 'Northerners' ate chip butties. If the nickname was meant to unseat me, it failed spectacularly, as I had never actually encountered a butty of any sort. I surmised that I must be some kind of posh Midlander/Northerner, but I had truly met my match down south. Admittedly, my dad said *Ey up me duck*, worshipped Brian Clough, and supported Nottingham Forest with a passion, but the extent of my Midlands persona involved asking for 10p scraps in a chip shop and knowing what a pikelet was.

I was not a typical public-school boy. From a very young age I remember being obsessed with music. My mother appeared to have a passion for Bill Haley—which reached its height when, in 1956, at the age of eighteen, she went to see the film *Rock Around The Clock* at the cinema—that subsequently developed into a love for Bread, James Taylor, and The Carpenters, but my father was always into Frank Sinatra, big-band jazz, and more big-band jazz. And as much as I love The Carpenters—and, believe me, there is no finer singer in the world than Karen Carpenter—I think it was my father's steadfast refusal to embrace any music that wasn't within his own strict remit that persuaded me that I wanted to find my own kind of music and become passionate when talking about it. One day, I would describe my profession (in an *i-D* magazine interview) as 'a music taste evangelist': I was trying to say that we all know taste is meant to be *personal*, but when someone says they like Cliff Richard, don't you want to say, 'Yes, I've heard many songs by Cliff Richard, but I have also heard many songs by Sonic Youth,

The Velvet Underground, Teenage Fanclub, and The Carpenters. And I have chosen the latter. Now, fuck off'?

My sister Michele and I were enamoured with the sounds of Radio 1 and Radio Luxembourg in the early 1970s, but I have to admit she was more Dave Lee Travis and Tony Blackburn than I ever was. This was surely due to our age difference—she is three years older—and she made her cool up in other ways. I wouldn't have developed an acquiescent fondness for Elton John, Supertramp, and Nazareth if it wasn't for her, and without her I would never have purchased my first three records: the Slade seven-inch single 'Gudbuy T' Jane' and their revelatory *Slade Alive* album, and a compilation album called *20 Power Hits* released on K Tel in 1973. Herein, I found my record taste endorsed by the authorities: Suzi Quatro, Mungo Jerry, Free, Clifford T Ward, Elton John, and The Carpenters were artists I had encountered before—most of the time on *Top Of The Pops*—but I felt exonerated to find them together on one collection. Several years later, I would be listening to Stuart Henry's *Street Heat* on Radio Luxembourg, and John Peel (under the bedclothes) on Radio 1 (whilst taping both), and I'd left my sister's musical environs behind.

At Sherborne School I stood on desks mimicking Headmaster MacNaughton, who sounded not unlike a particularly tight-arsed Winston Churchill, thus making the impression that much easier. Subsequently, when I was asked what made bread rise, or where the Somerset Hoare family lived, I'd answer *dynamite* or *Whore House* with such efficient endeavour that whichever school chums

I had conned into liking me would double up with laughter immediately. My most notorious pun, however, involved my own given surname and the morning register. Each day, the process would be repeated with monotonous regularity.

'Savidge?'

'Here, Sir.'

'Shaw?'

'Positive, Sir.'

I never tired of this routine. Nor did my fellow students, who never failed to congratulate me on the success of the punch line. Morning registration came and went, and yet still I persisted. It was only Shaw's transferral to another school that stopped the practice altogether.

My parents had helped transport my record collection, as well as my collection of *New Musical Express* magazines, to Sherborne, but very few boys seemed impressed. This was hardly the intention, but it would have been nice to know that punk and new wave had made some kind of dent outside of the metropolises. My father carried the last of my Clash, Jam, Stranglers, and Siouxsie & The Banshees records down a corridor and into my dormitory, and the formality generated by the other boys seemed palatable. My father didn't notice anything untoward, although perhaps his turn of phrase indicated that something was awry. 'Try not to get any girls pregnant,' he whispered when we were alone, and although I thought this rather crude—bordering on misogynist—at the time, I wonder now whether 'always wear a condom' might have seemed even more shocking—although this would have avoided the implication that he didn't really care about the girls and their pregnancies, just the inconvenience it might cause him. Of course, it's possible that I might have taken his advice literally and started wearing a condom at every available opportunity—in the shower, on the rugby field, during exams—but that was a chance he'd have to take. He'd once caught me staring at girls out of the car window and, when I looked embarrassed, suggested, 'There's nothing wrong with looking, son. If you weren't looking I'd be worried,' so it seemed like he had a phrase for every occasion. 'I've pissed my pants, Dad,' I might have said, and he would have replied, 'Don't worry, son, you haven't lived unless you've pissed your pants.'

But why hadn't he come up with 'try not to get your heart broken'? This would have suggested some sensitivity on his part, or at least an acknowledgement that I was a sensitive soul myself. I mean, who did he think he was packing off to school—Errol Flynn? No, I like to think his protestations said more about him than they did about me: if he told me not to impregnate females willy-nilly then he was basically saying that this is the kind of thing he would have got up to himself, given half the chance. And if he suggested that he didn't want to catch me *not* looking at girls out of the car window, it meant there'd be nothing odd about him looking at them himself.

My father was well known for his collection of eccentric phrases. I say *well known*, but it's conceivable that he only ever said them in front of me, and the rest of the world remained unaware of their existence. 'It's not a fashion parade, we're only going to Yeovil' was one of his favourites, trotted out whenever I seemed to be taking longer than fifteen minutes searching for the right jumper. 'Why do you need to go to London for new trousers? They've got perfectly good trousers in Wincanton' was another. The latter seemed downright nonsense, since *Come to Wincanton—we've got trousers* was not a slogan that would have been immortalised by the Wincanton Tourist Board.

My most treasured of his pronouncements, however, was uttered when I'd gone away to university and offered him a cup of Earl Grey tea as refreshment after his long drive. Step forward, 'I haven't got time for experiments', and claim your prize. Years later, in what passes for insider humour in the journalist fraternity, *Q* magazine would run my father's catchphrases down their masthead as a means of catching my attention, and perhaps an acknowledgement of their unique truth.

It is hardly surprising that Sherborne lacked musical cool—a few boys liked Bowie and Iggy, but the closest anyone else got to anything 'contemporary' was the progressive pretensions of Yes and Emerson Lake & Palmer—but at least it helped me to form my first real band and dream about becoming a pop star. Several years later, this is presumably how Coldplay sprang to life at Sherborne, but for me it was all about being as *moderne* as possible. And, yes, this included being pretentious as well. We failed miserably—at being pop stars, not at being pretentious or *moderne*—and our Victim Of Rhythm and Aural Sekts monikers should tell you everything you need to know about how far we were away from the zeitgeist. But at least we were real and had actual band members—in contrast to the band I formed in my bedroom at the age of fourteen, featuring me on drums (pillows), yours truly on twangy bass (clever tongue movements), me again on twangy guitar, and yes, you guessed it, that must have been me again on lead vocals.

My *Not Really A Band* was called Jimmy & The Dreadnoughts, and 'we' made our demo tape by recording drum/pillow slapping noises into a tape recorder, then playing this back whilst singing over the top and recording the whole thing into another tape recorder. This process would then be repeated, with twangy guitar and bass noises overlaid into the first tape recorder, presumably in the knowledge that this wasn't a million miles away from how The Beatles went about their first recordings.

Jimmy & The Dreadnoughts did not sign a record deal—how could we? We never left my bedroom—although I sometimes dreamt of our appearance on the John Peel show. 'That was a new song by Jimmy & The Dreadnoughts,' Peel would mutter in his finest dulcet tones. 'They're from a place called Ockbrook, just outside Derby, and they're made up of Jimmy Dread on lead vocals, Rachel Prejudice on twangy guitar, Suzie Dread on drums, and Molly Dread on twangy bass. You can catch them live in Jimmy's bedroom tomorrow night, and their debut album, *Do The Dread*, will be released next week on Dreadnought Recordings.'

Four years later, when I formed my first band containing more than one human being, we were fashionably New Romantic and counted Human League and Depeche Mode amongst our influences. You can bet I was primarily interested in the makeup, but Victim Of Rhythm did not embrace the miserabilism I craved, and songs like 'Young German In England' and 'Zero Gravity Sex' belied our innocent origins. *Zero Gravity Sex?* I'd never had any kind of sex. The band did supply me with my name, however. One morning, in rehearsals—we were that good!—I was making my passable impression of a drummer when one of my bandmates suggested that I had a tendency to pull a face like Filthy Phil of Motörhead. Whilst noting they'd mentioned my facial expression ahead of my heavy metal drumming prowess, I agreed that I wouldn't mind being called Phill—with two *L*s, and no mention of Filth.

The Phill name stuck, and I carried it with me to university. I chose Nottingham, since I'd never experienced the city as an adult, and, as a subject, philosophy, as I'd heard 40 percent of philosophy graduates were unemployed: what better excuse could I have suggested when I ultimately failed to secure a job? But Nottingham had also been chosen for an altogether different reason: it had the highest suicide rate of any university in Britain. If you coupled this with the knowledge that philosophy boasted the highest suicide rate of any degree course available, then you can see why my parents would think I was contemplating some kind of major self-harm. But what they failed to realise was that there was no *logical* reason why my doing philosophy at Nottingham entailed that I was going to kill myself. Indeed, a short glance at the statistics would have told them that Nottingham's philosophy department had suffered few suicides in recent years, and that they should have been far more concerned if I had embarked upon an architecture course. Naturally, it's impossible to explain this to elderly, immediate relatives with an unsound grasp of elementary logic.

I was, as you can see, at this not remotely tender age, an annoyingly contradictory teenager. And, soon, not even to be a teenager. My name, however, was not the only thing I'd brought with me to university; I'd also brought my First Proper Girlfriend. Well, when I say, *brought*, I should point out that my First Proper Girlfriend and I had started seeing each other whilst I was at Sherborne, and we'd decided to pursue a long-distance relationship when I moved to Nottingham. She, in turn, moved to London to study makeup technique at Steiner Beauty College. This proved to be an interesting development.

Once I was settled at university, I started to visit my girlfriend in her flat in the richly alien netherworld of Chelsea every other weekend. She used to have to practice her makeup techniques for several hours a day, and I was amazed at the amount of bags of makeup she had lying around the place. One day, she suggested it would be useful for her purposes to practice on me. For no particular reason, I agreed.

My girlfriend was already extremely expert at applying makeup, and I was quite feminine anyway, so, after an hour's application, I looked in the mirror and was astonished at the transformation. I looked completely female. She then suggested it would be

17

interesting if I dressed in her clothing, to see if I actually looked like a woman whilst wearing the makeup she had applied. I said I didn't mind, and together we selected an outfit comprising a short green three-tiered skirt and a white blouse that she had actually worn the day before. We matched this with tights and suede ankle boots that were, I assure you, fashionable at the time. I hated the outfit, but my girlfriend found the transformation so amusing that she asked me whether I would like my hair to be arranged into a style that would make me appear even more feminine. I feigned boredom before agreeing that this was the best course of action.

At about 9pm that evening, we were intently discussing how remarkable it was that I now looked so feminine when I suddenly blurted out, 'Wouldn't it be crazy if I walked round the block to see if anyone notices that I am not actually a woman?'

'That sounds like fun!' said my girlfriend, and within a few minutes, I had left her apartment and was walking around the square in close proximity. No one seemed to take the slightest bit of notice. When I arrived back, she asked how I had fared, and I told her that I had garnered absolutely no undue attention. Half an hour later, after neglecting to change my attire, I suggested I should venture out again. She had no objection—indeed, she was as fascinated by my success at looking so feminine as I was, and I think particularly proud of her efforts in this regard—and I was soon walking around the square again, this time making a point of passing near street lighting so that I could be properly noticed. Eventually, at some point in my travels, I managed to gather the confidence to enter a shop and browse for nothing in particular. Again, at no point did my appearance attract unwanted gaze.

Amateur transvestism notwithstanding, my relationship with my First Proper Girlfriend lasted a further three months before she ran out of makeup and moved on. I neglected my studies and concentrated on seeing as many live bands as I could. Nottingham's Rock City became my venue of choice; I saw Thompson Twins, Tears For Fears, Talk Talk, and Blancmange, before realising I preferred bands like Bauhaus, Echo & The Bunnymen, Killing Joke, Psychedelic Furs, Death Cult, Xmal Deutschland, Sex Gang Children, Danse Society, and Sisters Of Mercy, all of whom I saw at Rock City under various states of distressed undress. Perhaps inevitably, though not inadvertently, I became a goth, figuring that this was the best way for me to assimilate into regular society. I had a friend now, too: Jonathan, who was a fellow philosophy student, but far cooler than I could ever be—he had a nose ring and shaved hair like Annabella from Bow Wow Wow, and he'd already seen Death Cult in their original Southern Death Cult incarnation back in his home town, Lancaster. I could only dream of such sound indie-goth credentials. His dad had also been John Lennon's best pal back at art school, so that made him intimately connected to music royalty.

Jonathan and I spent most of our first year getting drunk, taking speed, missing lectures, and buying everything we read about in the *NME* in a record store called Selectadisc. Selectadisc was effortlessly, intimidatingly cool, and when I discovered, whilst rifling through my collection, that I'd lost my vinyl copy of The Clash's first album, I had to ask another student to go into Selectadisc and buy me another copy, so that the shop assistants wouldn't think I had never owned it in the first place. Jonathan and I laughed when our new friend dashed back to my car and handed us the replacement; we'd got away with it.

We saw The Smiths—and yes, it changed our lives—but we also saw Johnny Thunders out of morbid curiosity. Jonathan was already playing 'You Can't Put Your Arms Around A Memory' to death whilst learning the bass parts, and we both loved The New York Dolls and The Heartbreakers, but Johnny coming to Nottingham? It was like a spaceship landing in the quad. I bleached my hair blonde, then persuaded some girls to weave thirty horse plaits into it, before donning mascara, eye shadow, and lipstick and heading off to Rock City. Clearly, I just wanted to be Siouxsie Sioux—I had hundreds of black-and-white pictures of my idol cut out from the *NME* and Sellotaped onto my bedroom wall—but it was probably the wrong look for a Johnny Thunders crowd. At the gig itself, Johnny was more than an hour late, and when he came on stage he slurred his words, forgot his guitar parts, and stumbled around for a while before just about mumbling *I'm so alone* into the microphone. Then he collapsed to the floor, and it was all over.

After the gig, in the fish-and-chip shop, I ordered my food and became acutely aware of the smell of stale beer and fags behind me. I turned around and came face to face with three men who had definitely not been to see Johnny Thunders that evening. Maybe they'd been to the football, I don't know, but I could tell they didn't like me or the way I looked; one of them punched me in the mouth, and I banged my head on the fish counter. Jonathan ran out of the shop, and I crouched on the ground, feeling my mouth.

'You're a fookin' poof,' shouted the man who'd hit me, before kicking me in the knees. As I lay sprawling on the floor I could taste sweet blood pouring out of my mouth and I scrambled to my feet and ran for the door. The man tried to run after me but his two mates pulled him back and I got away. Halfway down the street, I caught up with Jonathan.

'Thanks for running away,' I said, not at all seriously.

'Well, what did you expect me to do?' he said. He was right; there was nothing he could have done. 'Have you seen your face?' he added, producing a compact. I took the compact off him and stared at my face. I looked awful: the man had punched me so hard that my tooth had come through my lip.

* * *

Naturally, my Rock City adventures continued throughout my tenure at university, but I knew I'd finally flown the family nest when I decided to stay on during the long, ten-week summer holiday in order to find a job. My fellow students were adamant that a lengthy stint *in situ* would demonstrate my independence, but a temporary job stacking shelves was not for me. I didn't fancy dealing with the general public—who does?—and the thought of stuffing envelopes for the *Daily Express* (an opportunity I'd read about on the house notice board) filled me with dread. However, I put the word around, and I was soon offered a position in the pastry department of a pork pie factory called Pork Farms.

Pork Farms was housed in a shambolic collection of buildings on an industrial estate on the edge of the city, and my 10pm start time meant that an air of foreboding surrounded the premises. It had felt rather glamorous, leaving all my friends in the pub about an hour earlier—like the hero of a gritty, northern, industrial novel heading off to the trenches—but as I approached the front gates I felt as nervous as if I was attending my first day at school. I introduced myself to the foreman, who handed me a clocking-in card—something I had only ever seen in *Carry On* or Boulting Brothers movies. This, I supposed, was what real people did for a living.

Everyone who worked in the Pork Farms pastry department had a criminal record. There was *Five Years*, who surprisingly had spent five years in prison for armed robbery, and there was *Baseball Bat*, who'd done time for hitting someone with a baseball bat. I can't remember if these were names I gave them or whether we all referred to each other in this way during friendly conversation. I was nicknamed *Brains*, since I was a university student, and I got the impression that I was being examined during every minute of my eight-hour shift.

During one shift, *Five Years* approached me and said he'd seen me driving to work that evening. He asked me whether I could give him a lift home.

'But you live completely in the opposite direction,' I said. 'I'd have to drive through town and then drive back through town.'

'I don't care,' he said menacingly, producing a knife as if it was the most normal thing in the world. 'I want a lift home.'

When I finished work, at 6am, I attempted to slip away quietly, but *Five Years* was way ahead of me.

'Come on then,' he said, slapping me on the back harder than was necessary. 'Let's go.'

We clocked out together, and he followed me to the car, which I'd parked on a nearby estate.

'Right,' said *Five Years*. 'I want you to drive to the end of this road as fast as you can, then turn 'round and drive back here as fast as you can. Then I want you to drive 'round the estate in third gear, and when I say *Now!* I want you to do a handbrake turn.'

I had no idea what he was talking about, but I decided to do exactly as he said. I drove to the end of the road as fast as I could, braked hard, turned, and completed exactly the same operation on the way back. Then I drove around the estate in third gear.

Suddenly, *Five Years* shouted *Now!* and banged his hand on the car dashboard. I jumped into a handbrake turn and sped off in the opposite direction.

'That was fookin' brilliant,' he said. 'You're a fookin' great driver. I'll tell you what: we're doing a job next week, and we really need someone on standby, to get us away if something goes wrong. What you doing a week on Friday?'

'I don't know,' I said. 'I'll have to have a think about it.'

23

I did have a think about it—for about five seconds—whilst I dropped *Five Years* off at the edge of the estate; it turned out that he didn't want a lift home after all. The next day I drove into work, leaving my car so far away from Pork Farms that I may as well have left it at home. When I arrived, *Five Years* was waiting for me.

'What's wrong wiv yer fookin' car?' he said.

'It's fooked,' I retaliated, in my finest Nottingham accent.

'Shame,' said *Five Years*.

And that was that.

Evidently, if I didn't own a functional car then I couldn't be considered for the job a week on Friday.

I finished my summer stint at Pork Farms without losing any teeth, and when term-time duties resumed, Jonathan and I formed a band. By the time 1984 ended, we'd become obsessed with R.E.M.—the band played Rock City in November that year, and we'd started buying as many live bootlegs of their output as possible—and it's possible that we just wanted to sound exactly like them. We drove to R.E.M. gigs all over the country and slept in my car whilst waiting for the band to arrive, all the time listening to my car stereo and trying to work out what Michael Stipe was singing on songs like 'Harbourcoat', 'Pretty Persuasion', and 'Sitting Still'. When it came to plucking up the courage to be my band's lead vocalist, I just didn't have it in me, so I stuck to drumming. It would be several months before we played live.

My lack of confidence in my musical endeavours was mirrored in other artistic pursuits; for some reason I had ambitions to be an actor, so I took parts in two student films I'd heard were in production. In one, I played the part of a Yugoslavian diplomat called Jaroslav Kubin—really just an excuse to wear an overcoat like Ian McCulloch and mumble incoherently into a hidden microphone. I was, no doubt, dreadful. For my second movie role, *Where Is She Now, Babe*, I played a rent boy to my pimp, Vivian MacKerrell, director Bruce Robinson's ex-housemate and the real-life inspiration for the Withnail character in *Withnail & I*. Vivian was living in Nottingham as he wanted to be near his daughter— at the time, I didn't quite understand the concept of fathers and mothers loving their children so much that they wanted to be near them even when they had left home—and I thought him the most charming, gentle soul who'd somehow lost his way and been reduced—*I'm a trained actor reduced to the life of a bum*—to accepting bit parts in dodgy films with the likes of me. He could act and I couldn't, so the whole thing seemed somewhat pointless.

Somehow, after this debacle, I was offered the lead part in a university play about suicidal young men. I was to play an imprisoned drug addict with suicidal tendencies, and I found I really could act, remember my lines, and interact successfully with my fellow actors. I also discovered that rehearsals didn't have to be arguing matches but could be an integral part of the learning process. Was it possible that I could be an actor after all?

And then I would remember that, at the end of the rehearsal period, I was expected to appear on a stage in front of a real live audience who would be hanging onto my every word.

I finished my philosophy degree and took a job at Selectadisc. Here I was able to indulge my vinyl fetish and buy every new twelve-inch single and album by Felt, The Replacements, New Order, and The Fall, several weeks before they were officially released. I could write *hippie goth shit* on the stickers on a Fields Of The Nephilim album, laugh at Numanoids who were looking for Gary Numan albums he'd signed in pencil—they'd come from Birmingham, where they'd bought the ones he'd signed in pen— and play 'difficult', noisy bands like Spaceman 3 to annoy the owner, Brian Selby.

'Phill,' Brian would say. 'People are actually leaving the shop.'

'Don't worry,' I said. 'They don't know what's good for them. They'll be trying to buy this stuff next week when we've sold out.'

This was the era of *formatting* to enhance your climb up the charts—Big Country had seven different formats for one release— and buying into the upper echelons meant record company reps tempting us with two-for-one deals on the latest hyped acts. We were cool and independent, so we were a hard nut to crack, but it would have been disingenuous to ignore their efforts entirely; instead, we went along with their offers but failed to pass the concessions on to the customer. By this method we managed to sell all our stock at the same price, thus protecting our favourite bands from oblivion.

The DJ Graeme Park worked in Selctadisc in those days, and he used to get sent the first house records from Detroit, New York, and Chicago. He started playing these in the shop—something I didn't fully appreciate at the time—and then at the Garage (a club also owned by the Selectadisc proprietor) in Nottingham, before moving to the Hacienda, where he became a pioneer of, and one of the biggest names in, dance music. Back then I took about as much notice of dance music as I did of the latest format revolution—CDs. Indeed, on one unremarkably momentous day, Brian made the decision to open a CD-only department in the store, and my co-workers Stuart and Neil (who would later unite to form the band Tindersticks) were commandeered to run the operation. When Stuart mentioned he was off to *CD Land*, I was strangely indifferent, confident that they would never catch on.

'Good luck with that, mate,' I said, glancing around at my own department, where customers were barely able to move.

Adverts for CDs were on TV already—they involved someone spreading jam on a CD and then jumping up and down on the afflicted item, thus proving their infallibility—but when I snuck down to Stuart's CD emporium later that day, the room was deserted. This was hardly surprising as, at this point, only three bands had CDs on the market: Dire Straits, Pink Floyd, and Genesis. Talk about Hobson's choice.

Of course, when I tried to check up on their department a week later, I had to abandon the task due to the number of customers—and artists—who'd switched over to the new format. *Suckers*, I thought, and then saw Stuart beaming from behind the counter. I returned to my section of the shop, somewhat bemused by the new order of things.

I still had my play, however, and I continued with rehearsals most evenings. I worked at the shop every day, but I could feel the tension building as knocking-off time approached; soon, I would have to leave the relative anonymity of working in a place I loved, to step out onto a stage where people would be looking at me.

I resolved to quit the play no matter how much embarrassment it caused. I would invent a job offer in London and say that I was considering my options. I dropped a few hints with the production team, and then, one day, when the director and I were alone, I blurted out, 'I've decided to take that job in a record shop in London. I'm sorry, but it's just such a great opportunity.'

'That's a real pity,' said the director. 'Well, the music business's gain is the acting fraternity's loss.'

No it's not, I thought, *because if I ever get as far as opening night, my stage fright is going to ruin your entire life*. But I agreed with his diagnosis and set about working out how I was going to avoid him on the streets of Nottingham for the next few years. And then, in a moment of terrible inspiration, the answer came to me: I would actually move to London.

I handed in my notice at Selectadisc, painfully conscious of the fact that I was now resigning myself to a life of buying records at full price. *The music business's loss*, I hear you scream. My final record-shop task involved selecting the song I would play as my Selectadisc epitaph. As a kind of *thank you, fuck you*, I chose REO Speedwagon's 'Keep On Loving You'.

America, you will never know how difficult it is to love this song. But I did and I do.

CHAPTER 2

LUNCH WITH THE WILD FRONTIERS

"When my mum first heard that I was somehow involved with Simple Minds—which I somehow wasn't—she started to cut out *Daily Telegraph* reviews of their performances and send them to me in the post."

During the not particularly hot or long summer of 1987, I boarded a National Express coach from Nottingham to London and found myself crawling through the window of a PR company called Ten Times Better. I was now the proud recipient of a philosophy degree and playing drums in a band called Kill Devil Hills. Yes, that's where the Wright Brothers made their inaugural flight—and, yes, we were *flying* musically. The band's manager, Ian Dickson—who subsequently went on to be Australia's version of Simon Cowell—was dating a woman (whom he later married) called Mel Bell, who ran the aforementioned PR company, and he had an idea that we should surprise her by climbing through her office window. She wasn't particularly amused by this jape, but after she had recovered from the initial shock of thinking I was the lead singer of Depeche Mode (I was wearing makeup and had also been mistaken for Adam Ant and Boy George in previous weeks) she decided that the best thing I could do was to type up a press release. She handed me some handwritten notes, and as I stabbed at the typewriter's keys—drunkenly and indiscriminately, as it turned out—I managed to change the hapless scribble into something quite decent.

The next morning, Mel called me and said she'd *never read anything like it*. She also confessed she'd had a dream we were going to work together. She asked whether I'd be interested.

'Not really,' I said, but perhaps if she got rid of the rest of her staff, as the short time I'd spent with them had convinced me that they were all idiots. Oh, and if she let me use the company headed paper to represent Kill Devil Hills. Amazingly, she agreed, and Mel Bell Publicity was born.

In the early days, Mel and I found it tough, since we could hardly afford the rent for our second-floor office on the Mile End Road, and central heating was out of the question. But somehow or other, after a few weeks, we managed to get short-term contracts with Gaye Bykers On Acid, Danielle Dax, and comparatively unknown US independent record labels like Homestead and Reachout International Records. Looking after Homestead and ROIR—the former had early recordings by Sonic Youth and Dinosaur Jr; the latter was a cassette-only label featuring live performances by The Beastie Boys, Television, and The New York Dolls—meant that I could begin to nurture a love/hate relationship with the *New Musical Express*, *Melody Maker*, *Sounds*, and *Record Mirror*, at least one of which I would have died to write for at the time. This 'relationship' was almost certainly nothing to do with my nascent PR credentials, so it must have been because wilfully obscure acts like Big Dipper, Nice Strong Arm, Live Skull, Butthole Surfers, and Daniel Johnston were always going to appeal to journalists who wanted to let the public know they'd heard something they couldn't possibly know anything about otherwise. It was hardly The Tubes screeching '*I was a punk before you were a punk*', but I had learned a PR truth nonetheless.

Perhaps, however, when I come to think about it, it's entirely feasible that the *inkies*—as we used to call them in those days—appreciated our cute ambivalence for the simple reason that we were small and independent; habitually, they were desensitised to phone calls from publicists at EMI and Sony, who didn't seem to care in the way that we did, and it must have been a breath of fresh air when we turned up in person with our twelve-inch test pressings and cassette copies of singles and albums. I remember sending *Melody Maker*'s Everett True a Daniel Johnston *Hi, How Are You* T-shirt, the album having just been released on Homestead; Everett gave it to Kurt Cobain, and Kurt later wore it in just about every subsequent photo session. I also remember a copy of the *NME* being biked to our shitty offices most weeks because we couldn't actually afford to travel into town to buy it. Out of this charming ignominy we graduated to sitting in the *NME* editorial offices every other week, just so we could get them to listen to records we liked. This didn't seem unusual at the time: they'd just ask what we'd got and then nod or shake their heads accordingly.

As part of the Homestead deal we got GG Allin thrown in. Allin was a self-styled, self-mutilating, rock'n'roll fuck-up whose unlistenable dirge I'd somehow got confused with Frank Zappa and Iggy Pop—you know, shitting on stage and cutting your arms up for a laugh. We'd received two hundred copies of his latest record in the office, but it wasn't until I'd mailed out fifty of them that I got around to reading the lyric sheet. The guy was seriously deranged, and his lyrics advocated the brutal rape and murder of women. I quickly drafted a letter to all the fifty journalists who'd received the record and implored them not to review it. The letter worked and only one review of the record appeared. I realise now that this was because the journalist thought I was being postmodern.

I burned the rest of the albums in the back garden—producing an awfully pungent odour and a terrible black fog—and then told the record company that everyone hated the record. This was to become a recurring theme throughout my early career in PR—and not a million miles away from William Fisher flushing calendars down the loo in Keith Waterhouse's *Billy Liar*—as it's an easy way of diverting blame from your own feeble efforts. *The singer's ugly and his lyrics are sexist?* If the press don't notice—since you neglected to send them the records in the first place—you tell the manager and the A&R guy that the press *have* noticed, and we're all going home with the afternoon off. Chances are the (usually male) manager and A&R guy haven't read the lyrics anyway, and the pair are not going to deny the singer's unattractiveness in case you think they're gay.

My spell with Mel Bell ensured I was able to understand how PR functioned. Or didn't function. After the GG Allin fracas, Mel and I began to represent two young girls from Leeds called The Rhythm Sisters, and somehow I managed to persuade *Vogue* magazine to run a feature on them. The photo shoot, in a fashionably distressed region of Kings Cross, also meant that I became familiar with the casual ephemera associated with the arena they call *public relations*.

At the end of the photo shoot—orchestrated by someone called Jonathan Le Bon, who may or may not have been the brother of Duran Duran's Simon—The Rhythm Sisters and I were dismissed to go back to our respective environments. As the makeup artists, stylists, flower arrangers, catering providers, photographer's assistants, and indeed photographers themselves vacated the premises, I decided to remain, so that I could observe the leftover remnants of the typical PR shoot—and miss the rush-hour tube home. As I shuffled amongst the discarded makeup, the uneaten debris of several exotic fruits I would never know the name of, and sandwiches that could only ever be available via an unlisted catering service, I realised I was now alone, and the entire exorbitant display was going to waste. What was I to do? Well, I'll tell you: this poor, beleaguered press officer took those items back to the small, sad, twentieth-floor apartment of his tower-block 'complex' in Bow, East London.

And he kept the makeup.

The *Vogue* shoot was hardly indicative of my daily PR routine. Indeed, most of my working day seemed to consist of making up stories and trying to place them in the gossip columns of the four main weekly music magazines. It was all I could do to spin stories about Danielle Dax, a gorgeous female goth artist who I was vaguely in love with—although I was more in love with the possibility of looking like her—but when a guy called Charlie Cosh called and offered to pay us £50 a week to make up stories about a band called The Shamen, we readily agreed. This, I concluded, would allow our imaginations to run wild.

Subsequently, I invented a story about The Shamen's transit

van careering off the motorway, and all copies of their new twelve-inch single being destroyed in the ensuing melee. 'If anyone manages to track down a copy in a record shop,' I'd venture, 'they'll know they've got their hands on a rare beast indeed, and possibly something worth a great deal more than what they'd originally paid out.' Other stories included reports that the band were haunted by spirits who added noises and sounds to their records without their knowledge—which could only be discovered if one checked out the commercially available product.

In some ways, these were the perfect gossip-column stories: no one was injured or offended, and it is possible that people were genuinely motivated to track down Shamen records after reading them. Although I've yet to meet anyone who did.

Around this time, the band I secured most coverage for were called Gaye Bykers On Acid. Undoubtedly, they were all legally mad, but their name allowed them some leeway in this regard, and the fact that they were fronted by a guy called Mary Byker meant that I forgave them anything. I envied his name enormously. They were heavily involved in the Grebo scene, a movement that comprised other East Midlands–based acts like Pop Will Eat Itself, Zodiac Mindwarp, and Crazyhead. This was my first experience of a scene you could manipulate for your own evil media ambitions, and I leapt on every opportunity to attach Gaye Bykers to the movement, even though the band remained unmoved—and indeed dispirited—by my efforts. Their name was so intriguing, however, that it's entirely likely they would have made an impression without my input, but I can assure you it was far easier to get them noticed when you placed them next to several other bands with an apparently similar ideology.

My success with Gaye Bykers, Homestead, and, in particular, Green On Red—the latter was my first experience of securing a *Melody Maker* cover story—must have captured someone's attention, because I somehow heard there was a vacancy in the press office at Virgin Records, and that it would be in my interests to apply for the role. I discussed the offer with Mel, but it took three interviews before Virgin agreed to take me on. Perhaps, at the time, I was not traditional major-label press-officer material; I had blonde, spiky hair and six earrings, and when asked to name my favourite kind of music, I said the Sex Pistols, and even though the band had, at one point, been signed to the label for a significant amount of time, certain looks were exchanged. Nevertheless, my sense of righteousness prevailed.

On June 20 1988, I made my way from my twentieth-floor flat in Bow to the impressively grand Virgin Records building in Harrow Road. Naturally, I was spectacularly early, and when I arrived for my first day of work the building was deserted, apart from a receptionist, a security guard, and one or two personal assistants who had arrived ahead of their bosses in order to make preparations for the day. I parked my cheap Ford Cortina next to the managing director's Aston Martin and sauntered into the reception area, where I was guided in the general direction of the press office. I sidled down several corridors before settling on a terminally untidy room, the walls of which were covered in newspaper cuttings and framed front cover images of what I could only assume were several notable Virgin acts.

All the desks in the press office were draped with newspaper cuttings, ashtrays, cassettes, CDs, notebooks—presumably containing pertinent notes on other Virgin artists—and cardboard record-sleeve artwork. I walked around the office until I chanced upon an empty, forlorn-looking desk that I presumed to be reserved for newcomers.

On my desk—which appeared to be in a most undesirable position in the centre of the office, almost as if it had been placed there by the other press officers in a bid to make me feel as uncomfortable as possible—I noticed a diary, placed open on that day's date. I sat down behind the desk and imagined myself answering calls from important people in the media, all the while glancing at the diary in front of me. On the page before me, in large black felt letters, I read the announcement *LUNCH WITH THE WILD FRONTIERS*. I must have stared at that page for around ten minutes, trying to work out what the words meant. *Lunch with The Wild Frontiers?* Shouldn't it have said *Lunch IN The Wild Frontiers*, presumably because the Wild Frontiers was the name of a nearby restaurant or drinking establishment?

The room soon began to fill up with new work colleagues, and I introduced myself to anyone who cared to listen. After a suitable amount of time, I asked my new boss what the words in my diary could possibly mean, and she explained that *The Wild Frontiers* was the name of a band that I had been assigned to represent. I was to be picked up in their car at 12:30 and escorted to an Ethiopian restaurant, where we were to discuss the press campaign for their forthcoming single.

Whilst I was pleased to discover the true nature of the phrase in my diary, I was more than a little put out to realise that I was now expected to attend a restaurant serving Ethiopian food, as Ethiopia, the last time I'd looked, seemed to me to be under the effects of terrible starvation. This was not long after the Michael Buerk expose of the famine in Africa—and the subsequent Live Aid concerts—and I couldn't work out whether the Ethiopian restaurant ruse wasn't part of some terrible induction process that the Virgin Records press-office staff were now using on their new recruits. What if my presence at the restaurant caused a demonstration by anti-globalisation activists who saw me as a typical example of a privileged middle class, dining out for the purpose of fun and—my own—ironical amusement?

I attempted to dismiss my downbeat thoughts about the forthcoming lunch for the rest of the morning, so that I could concentrate on more important matters—namely, what other artists I would be assigned to represent in my first few months at the company. I already knew I was lucky enough to look after the mysterious Wild Frontiers, but who else?

Developments at the morning's PR scheduling meeting—my first proper meeting about anything, ever—were not encouraging: apparently, I was to be charged with representing a band called It

Bites—an arrogant, pretentious progressive-rock outfit fronted by a guy called Francis Dunnery, who thought he was The Second Coming. Of course, I could hardly be aware of their full musical illegitimacy at the time, but several meetings with the band in the next twelve months convinced me they were unworthy of my considered attention. On one occasion when I was in their company, they suggested they were particularly happy I was their press officer, since if I *was a bird*, I'd fancy them; on yet another occasion, they were discussing an at-the-time unsubstantiated rumour that Prince's backing singers, Wendy & Lisa—who had just signed to Virgin—might be lovers, concluding that the possibility was *disgusting*.

I had not encountered such unreconstructed male behaviour since my school days in the 70s, and I began to plan ways I could humiliate them in public. Subsequently, this would involve telling journalists to express their true opinions when they attended the band's concerts, and to ask the band questions that I knew would reveal the true nature of their idiocy. This 'unprofessional' behaviour, which surely can't have been replicated by anyone else in my position—ladies and gentlemen, I was a pioneer even in those days—might be seen as disingenuous, but, when you really think about it, what was I actually doing wrong? The band were so far up their own arses you'd have to employ several members of Yes and Emerson Lake & Palmer (yes, it was nice to see those recalcitrant bedfellows once again) to surgically remove their egos—so all I could really be guilty of was leading innocent critics

LUNCH WITH THE WILD FRONTIERS

to their prey. One or two might comment, 'Phill. Are you sure?' To which, I would retort, 'Yes. For the sake of reason and good sense, please let the people know the truth.'

Animal Logic (managed by Miles Copeland and featuring his younger brother, Stewart), Danny Wilson, Johnny Hates Jazz, When In Rome—I am sure these names mean something to some people, but was there ever a time when the fat, bloated excess of record company mismanagement conjured up such a cornucopia of misdeed? When I joined Virgin Records in the summer of 1988, there were 106 acts signed to the label; a year later, less than half of these had survived. Something had to give.

Which brings me to The Wild Frontiers.

At 12:30, a car arrived containing members of an unpopular musical combo. I climbed into the car and was introduced to several men sporting rockabilly haircuts and casual cowboy gear. One of them I recognised as Marco Pirroni, erstwhile lead guitarist of Adam & The Ants, and it suddenly hit me: Marco had been responsible for co-writing the hugely successful Adam & The Ants album *Kings Of The Wild Frontier*, and this, his new band, was presumably created to cash in on the notoriety generated by that chart-topping disc.

Marco and his slightly younger entourage of wannabe cowboys were charming enough but lacked charisma, and, when we arrived at the Ethiopian restaurant at the other end of Harrow Road, I soon became distracted. The food was exceptional, but as we handed around bowls of spicy stew—together with the band's first two singles on a cassette and the results of the band's latest photo session—I couldn't help wondering whether I might have had more fun if some anti-globalisation activists had actually deigned to join us.

Back in the office, I played the band's material—some kind of cod-garage-rockabilly—on the stereo whilst leafing through the photo session I'd been handed earlier. The music elicited little response from the rest of the office, although the photo session proved another matter entirely: several of my colleagues crowded around me and began to examine the contact sheets using magnifying glasses they'd picked up from their own desks and brought over to mine. They all seemed to know what they were doing, so I left them to it. Eventually, after a brief consultation between the others, four photographs were selected, and I was asked to call a reproduction house to order some prints. I ordered thirty of each, just to be on the safe side.

These were the days when Virgin boss Richard Branson used to turn up unannounced in order to drum up enthusiasm from his troops to get his records to no.1. I remember him coming in to the press office to tell us that Simple Minds were only no.2 in the midweek charts; if we spent all of the next day—Friday—packaging up a special new format to sell in to the shops on Saturday then, he assured us, the band would hit the no.1 spot.*

---

* When my mum first heard that I was somehow involved with Simple Minds—which I somehow wasn't—she started to cut out *Daily Telegraph* reviews of their performances and send them to me in the post. To this day, with varying regularity, she still calls me up to say, 'They're in the *Telegraph* again.'

'You've got some of the finest minds in the UK stooping to the level of warehouse skivvies?' I pointed out.

'Yes,' he replied.

'Fair enough,' I said, as I pushed another copy of the pompous drivel that was 'Belfast Child' into its impressively gate-folded sleeve. The record went to no.1.

Aside from The Wild Frontiers and It Bites, my first ever PR meeting threw up several more musical anomalies. I was to represent Suicidal Tendencies, a band I was already familiar with due to the song 'Institutionalized', which I'd encountered on a movie soundtrack some years earlier. With a name like Suicidal Tendencies and a reputation for releasing hard-core punk and thrash metal material, I was initially nervous about encountering their lead singer, Mike Muir, but I needn't have worried: we met and shook hands at the foot of the stairs in the entrance hall of the Columbia Hotel, and when I offered to buy him a drink he asked for a Diet Coke. Then, when we climbed into my car so that we could drive to the band's first UK photo session, I noticed that he strapped on his seat belt immediately; not only was this not a particularly common action at the time, it was also not the act one expected of someone who sang in a band called Suicidal Tendencies. Finally, when we discussed the band's music and what it meant to him, Muir turned to me and said, 'I just want to make enough money so I can get a house like my grandfather.'

This was the first time I realised they did things differently in America. No one in a rock band in the UK—at least in the heady daze before the crushing homogeneity of talent academies and *The X Factor* won out—would ever admit to wanting to own a house, let alone *a house like my grandfather*, and nor would they be allowed to get away with such a comment. In Britain, all the requirements you needed to be a rock star were that you couldn't play an instrument very well and you had no other ambitions other than to be a rock star.

And you had to look good.

But things weren't so bad: I also got given Gaye Bykers On Acid! That's right, those bunch of ne'er do wells had followed my defection to Virgin Records and signed on the dotted line shortly after my inauguration. I was more than a little thrilled, since I already knew how to conduct a press campaign on their behalf. However, the two albums they released—*Drill Your Own Hole* and *Stewed To The Gills*—failed to set the charts alight, and it was only their transformation into a band called Lesbian Dopeheads On Mopeds—where they dressed in drag and conducted phone interviews using falsetto voices—that proved the least bit entertaining: on the live front, this enabled the band to support themselves, thus ensuring they received payment twice, but it also enabled me to obtain twice the amount of press coverage.

Paradoxically, for some strange reason, in these early unfamiliar weeks, I was also mistaken for someone who liked world music. In the late 1980s, Virgin Records had created a subsidiary label called Earthworks that was forging a reputation for introducing the Western world to groundbreaking albums by artists such as

Youssou N'Dour, Mahlathini & The Mahotella Queens, Four Brothers, and Soul Brothers, and as I had heard of all of these I must have seemed like the most likely person to represent them on a professional basis. What I failed to point out at the time, however, was that I had heard their records on John Peel's late-night show and actually edited them out of the compilation tapes I made of his programme. It wasn't that I actively disliked them, it's just that they didn't sit next to the Fall, Smiths, Bogshed, and Woodentops tunes that I favoured at the time.

Whatever the reasons, I ended up looking after Earthworks and an album called *Rai Rebels*—a compilation album of various Rai musicians featuring Cheb Khaled, who seemed to be singing a song whose lyrics were translated to me as, '*Going out and getting pissed / Going out and getting pissed*.' I loved it to bits, as I did Youssou N'Dour, who, despite being dismissed as 'useless 'n dire' by *Melody Maker*, turned out to be the most delightful and charming man I had ever encountered. A year after his seminal *Immigrés* album release on Earthworks, Youssou would be collaborating—not for the first time—with Peter Gabriel on *Passion*, the soundtrack to Martin Scorsese's *The Last Temptation Of Christ* movie and the first Gabriel release on his new world-music label, Real World.

My experience with Earthworks, and my brief association with Youssou, must have stood me in good stead, because I was deemed *just the right person* to help publicise the launch of Real World. Gabriel chose Paris for the launch, but he also chose Rosanna

Arquette as his travelling companion, so it was with some excitement that I boarded a plane to Paris—with a journalist from *City Limits* magazine—to meet them both. Gabriel was dating Arquette at the time, and I was actually keener on meeting her than I was Gabriel; it'd only been four years since I'd seen her in *Desperately Seeking Susan* and fallen ever more deeply in love with her co-star, Madonna. The movie had inspired me to attempt to write a novel called *Madonna & Me*, featuring a boy who lives on the twentieth floor of a tower block in Bow, east London, but wakes up in a New York townhouse to find that he now inhabits the body of Madonna; correspondingly, Madonna wakes up in the body of the boy on the twentieth floor of a tower block in Bow, east London, and the pair's sole motivation soon becomes evident: each has to track down the other—through customs and security, in her case—with a view to being reunited with the correct physical anatomy. It was no doubt 'one hell of a yarn' (*New York Times*) and 'a brilliant retelling of Franz Kafka's Metamorphosis and a caustic satire on modern day celebrity' (*Times Literary Supplement*), but it was also a means of advertising my literary wares in front of Madonna, whom I knew to be something of an Anglophile. Perhaps Arquette would be able to effect an introduction?

In Paris, I made my way to a Peter Gabriel press conference already descending into chaos. France was not my territory, and I was required only to attend with one UK journalist, but when we arrived I could sense Gabriel's frustration. At least half the questions seemed to concern his relationship with Arquette, who was in attendance at the press conference but standing at the back of the room. When the questions on Real World dried up altogether and journalists started asking where Arquette was planning on shooting her next movie, Gabriel's resentment got the better of him and he called an end to proceedings. Soon afterwards, the pair left in a taxi for the hotel.

Back at the hotel, I spoke briefly to Peter and Rosanna before the latter departed for Cannes, where she was promoting her latest film. Sadly, the subject of *Madonna & Me* never came up. Peter promised that he would do his interview with *City Limits* magazine as soon as he had completed the set of interviews for the French press that the Virgin international department had organised. I ordered him a salad and myself a bottle of champagne.

Four hours later—after I'd consumed around four bottles of champagne—I checked in on Peter's progress, only to find him looking exhausted and insisting that he needed to get to the airport as soon as possible.

Shit, I thought. *I've forgotten to set up the interview.*

'Any chance you can do the interview in the cab on the way to the airport?' I asked hopefully.

'Hmm, I suppose so,' said Peter.

'Great,' I replied, and rushed back into the bar to let the *City Limits* journalist know he needed to leave for the airport immediately.

Some two hours later, the very same car would bring the *City Limits* journalist back to the hotel.

'That was a great interview,' he said. 'He answered every question.' *How could he not? He couldn't get away!*

By this time I'd paid the hotel bar bill: six thousand francs. Still, at least Peter had a salad.

On the way back to London, I listened to the cassette copy of *Passion* that Peter had handed to me in Paris. I now had a newfound love: not Bogshed but Nusrat Fateh Ali Khan. Just saying his name made me feel exotic. Several months later, *Passion* would be released on Real World, and Youssou, now signed to Virgin, would release *The Lion* to much fanfare. In June that year, the pair would appear together on the cover of the *New Musical Express*.

And The Wild Frontiers?

Within six weeks of signing to Virgin Records, they were dropped by the label. I managed to take receipt of one hundred and twenty ten-by-eight black-and-white shots of the band, but that's about it. The photographs stayed in my in-tray, gathering dust, my increasingly hectic and overstuffed diary appearing to mock the lack of activity surrounding them. No one rang me about them, no one wrote about them, and the presence of their name next to the title of their debut single on the label's scheduling material came to be seen as something of an in-house joke. I was not surprised when their name disappeared from our roster of bands. What is surprising, however, is that if you google *The Wild Frontiers*, you will find no mention of a band that was once signed to Virgin Records—even if it was only for six weeks.

You will also find no mention of them in any of Marco Pirroni's many musings on the subject of his music, nor on his Wikipedia page, nor even in the list of bands he has written and recorded with in the last thirty years. Is it possible that, rather like those who fell out of favour with Joseph Stalin in the early days of the Soviet Union, they have been airbrushed from history? Or could it be that they never existed in the first place, and I dreamt the whole thing up? Indeed, did I even go for lunch with them in an Ethiopian restaurant on the Harrow Road?

Reader, I assure you: I did.

CHAPTER 3

MYSTERY GIRL

"We shook hands, and I remember thinking that I was shaking the hand that had shaken Elvis Presley's hand on so many occasions. Which begs the question, when someone shakes my hand, are they shaking Elvis's hand or Roy's? The choice is yours!"

I was never Head Of Press at Virgin Records, but when I heard Barbara Orbison, wife and manager of Roy, was coming into the office I thought it necessary to act as if I was. Sian Davies, my boss at the time, was lunching elsewhere, and when Barbara arrived I just happened to be sitting in Sian's seat.

Barbara knocked expertly on the half-open glass door.

'Are you Sian?' she asked. 'I'm Barbara Orbison.'

'No,' I replied, standing up and reaching out my hand to greet her. 'I'm Phill. Very pleased to meet you. Please take a seat.' I gestured to the chairs dotted around the room.

Barbara was wearing a dark trouser suit, and I liked her immediately. I knew her to be of German origin, and she was certainly an impressive, beautiful woman. When she pulled up a chair and sat down, I explained that we were honoured to have Roy sign for the company, and we couldn't wait to start work on his new album, *Mystery Girl*, in earnest. She looked perplexed, but when I mentioned that I already had interviews lined up with the *NME*, *The Observer*, the *Mail On Sunday*, and *The Face*, her expression changed.

'When will Roy be available for interviews?' I asked.

'We can do some in the hotel early next week,' she replied. 'We're staying at St James's. Just let me know the schedule—not too early—and I'll go through everything with Roy.' She stood up and we shook hands again. As she left, I remember thinking that Roy was lucky to have so formidable an ally in his camp. Or in both camps, as it were.

When Sian came back from lunch, I told her that Barbara had been in and we'd talked about the forthcoming press campaign. I didn't tell her that the encounter had taken place in her office, or that Barbara seemed to be under the impression that I was running the operation. Sian seemed pleased that there was one less thing for her to deal with.

Of course, it didn't take long for Sian to find out what had happened, since Barbara had phoned someone high up at Virgin as soon as she'd left. 'I met our press person,' she must have said, 'and he's really nice and everything—although quite frankly I've never met anyone with six earrings and peroxide blonde hair before—but isn't he awfully young to be running a press department?'

'Don't worry about that,' came the reply, once he'd figured out what she was talking about, 'he's perfectly capable of being in charge.' And then he'd asked Sian to come and see him and explain what was going on.

But I got away with it. Sian assured Barbara that I was a huge Roy Orbison fan and the best person in the press department to represent him. And besides, the idea was to introduce Roy to a new generation, and I had all the contacts at the *NME* and *Melody Maker* and *The Face*. After some initial misgivings, Barbara just had to agree.

On the day of Roy's first press interview, I was so nervous I arrived at St James's two hours early and walked around the square, muttering to myself, whilst trying to work out the best time to officially *arrive*. Finally, I plucked up the courage to make myself known at reception. Barbara came downstairs, looking suitably demure, and I was ushered up to their room—or rooms—to meet the man himself. Roy was magnificent, resplendent in white dressing gown and wet hair arranged in a ponytail—by which I mean to say that he had obviously completely forgotten that I was coming to meet him. We shook hands, and I remember thinking that I was shaking the hand that had shaken Elvis Presley's hand on so many occasions. Which begs the question, when someone shakes my hand, are they shaking Elvis's hand or Roy's? The choice is yours!

Roy lit a cigarette—a Marlborough Red—and we discussed the interview that was due to take place over dinner that evening. He'd met the journalist from the *Mail On Sunday* on a previous occasion—and I hadn't—so that already made things awkward. At the restaurant, an Indian establishment in Marble Arch, I barely said a word, too young and out of my depth to share in the reminiscences of what seemed like a bygone age. I eyed the prices on the menu with trepidation, since I knew I had to pay for the meal as a representative of Virgin Records, but I ordered my food with the insouciance of someone with plain tastes who also happened to be on a diet. But I ate nonetheless; the only indication that I was nervous was my constant wrestling of banknotes in my jacket pocket. I was too young and not important enough to have a credit card, so I'd taken £400 out of the bank earlier that day, hoping that it would cover the cost of the meal.

Thankfully, the £400 was enough, and I survived the ordeal. Back in the office the following day, I received a phone call.

'Hi, is that Phill?' said the voice on the other end of the line. 'This is Derek. I run the Roy Orbison Fan Club, and I'd love to tell our members where to look out for Roy in the newspapers in the weeks to come.'

Derek had a delightful, elderly, avuncular Scottish brogue, and my heart warmed to him as he seemed to have only one goal in life—to promote the unique delights of Roy Orbison to anyone willing to listen. No doubt he should have been doing my job all along, but I suspected he had no job at all. Or perhaps he was retired, I didn't know.

Derek already knew that I'd had dinner with Roy, Barbara, and the *Mail On Sunday* the night before, and to this day I don't know how he was aware of our movements. He was very excited that the public were once again discovering his beloved Roy after so many years in the wilderness. Roy's 'In Dreams' had recently achieved huge notoriety after Dean Stockwell's spookily prescient lip-synch nailed the song in David Lynch's recently released movie *Blue Velvet*—Roy had actually told me how freaked out and yet flattered he had been by *that* unique reinterpretation; The Travelling Wilburys, of whom Roy, along with Bob Dylan, Tom Petty, George Harrison and Jeff Lynne, formed an integral part, had recently achieved both critical and commercial success; and the signs were extremely promising that the imminent release of Roy's solo album, *Mystery Girl*, would prove a watershed. The latter boasted songwriting credits by Bono and The Edge, Elvis Costello, Jeff Lynne, Tom Petty, Diane Warren, and Albert Hammond.

None of the exceptionally talented singer-songwriter detainees detailed above held as much lure for me, however, as the possibility that I was going to meet Nick Kent, my favourite journalist of all time, and a man I'd persuaded to interview Roy for *The Face*. He didn't take much persuading, mind you, and after I'd sent him a cassette of the new album he sent me a handwritten letter thanking me for the cassette and the opportunity to interview one of his heroes.

Nick had famously never owned a tape recorder, preferring to document interviews by writing everything down on the back of a fag packet, but when he turned up at the hotel for the second round of interviews, he was clutching a Sony Walkman he'd bought for the occasion. The thing was still in its cellophane, and he spent most of the next ten minutes trying to open it and then fiddling with the inordinate number of batteries he seemed to be carrying.

'It's only for Roy, man,' he rasped, drawing on his cigarette. 'I gotta get the whole thing down.'

Once Nick finally managed to get the Walkman and the batteries to be one giant working unit, we went upstairs to meet Roy in his suite. Roy was again dressed in his white dressing gown with his hair in a ponytail. I figured he must be dressed like this at all times of the day and night. Nick didn't seem at all put out by Roy's state of undress, although Roy apologised for not being correctly prepared and disappeared into another room to get changed into his proper clothing. When he returned, I asked Roy if he was comfortable doing the interview in the room, and when he said he was fine, I left them to it. As I closed the door, I took one last look at Nick fiddling with his tape recorder and wondered if he even knew how to switch the thing on.

Two hours later, Nick emerged into the lobby downstairs looking like he'd seen a ghost—or at least the man he had been waiting to meet his whole life. He thanked me again for the opportunity to interview Roy and said that he hoped to have the piece written up by the end of the following week. As we talked, he was clutching his tape recorder with such urgency that I wondered if he was expecting to be mugged; Nick had a chequered past with dealing with errant rock stars (including Sid Vicious and Adam & The Ants guitarist Matthew Ashman) who often took offence to his superbly barbed rhetoric, and it was entirely possible that he could be attacked in the lobby at any moment. When Nick saw me noticing this delicate, unusual movement, we both grinned (or did we grimace?) with mutual recognition.

Nick soon left, and I was hanging around in the lobby wondering what to do when Roy appeared.

'Hi Phill,' he said in his slight, Texan drawl. 'Who was that guy who just interviewed me?'

'Nick Kent,' I said. 'He's a legendary *NME* journalist who really knows his stuff and has always wanted to meet you.'

'Well, that was a really great interview,' said Roy. 'In fact, that was the best interview I've ever done. When you speak to him again, I'd like you to ask him whether he'd like to write the story of my life. I have so many offers from people who want to do my biography, but he was wonderful, wonderful. He asked me stuff I'd never been asked before.'

Suddenly, Barbara arrived, and she and Roy embraced. They spoke briefly, and I learned that they were both about to depart for different parts of the globe: Barbara was due to get on a plane to see her family in Germany whilst Roy was planning to fly to Henderson, Tennessee, at a later date so that he could be with his mother. They weren't going to be seeing each other until much later that month.

Barbara left for the airport in a cab, and I said goodbye to Roy and went back to the office. My phone was ringing as I sat down at my desk.

'Hello, it's Derek from the Roy Orbison Fan Club,' said Derek. 'I heard you did another interview at the hotel. How did it go? Do you know when it's going to be published?'

'It's going to be in the next issue of *The Face* magazine,' I replied. 'It should be out next month.'

'That's great,' said Derek. 'My mother will be really pleased.' Derek sounded as if he was at least seventy years old, so I wondered what his mother would make of *The Face*. Perhaps in the next few years she would become an admirer of Boy George or Neneh Cherry and start splinter fan clubs.

The following day, Roy did several more interviews at the hotel. It was late afternoon before we wrapped up proceedings, and as we said goodbye I felt a tinge of regret that I was leaving him alone without Barbara for companionship. He suddenly seemed old and somehow lonely. I never saw him again.

The following week, on Tuesday December 6 1988, Roy died of a massive heart attack at his mother's house in Hendersonville. I was driving to work when they announced his death on the eight o'clock news on Radio 1. I turned the radio up and there it was again: *Roy Orbison has died at the age of fifty-two*. They were playing 'Pretty Woman' so it must be true.

I pulled the car over into a side street and cried. I couldn't quite believe what I'd heard, but then I remembered something I'd read in a newspaper a few weeks back: anyone who's had triple heart-bypass surgery never survives more than ten years. And Roy's surgery had been in 1978.

I stayed in my car in the side street for around an hour before summoning up the energy to carry on driving to the office. When I arrived at the gates of Virgin Records' Kensal House, there was already a sea of flowers blocking my entrance. Evidently, word had spread very quickly. I parked around the corner.

It was a similar story when I got into the office: the receptionist was crying, and the reception area was awash with roses. Before I could make my way through to the press office, I bumped into Roy's A&R guy, who told me I needed to follow him into a staff meeting, where plans were afoot for an emergency course of action.

Everyone who'd been assigned to work on Roy's record was in the meeting, and a good deal of them appeared to have been crying. However, it didn't take long before someone suggested that it might not be such a bad thing that Roy had died, since it meant that he was now headline news and everyone would surely want to buy his new record. Several other people in the meeting nodded their heads in agreement, and a decision was reached to bring the release forward in order to capitalise on the attendant publicity generated by Roy's death.

I couldn't believe what I was hearing, and I resolved to get out of the meeting as quickly as possible. This was easily done, since I was the one who was going to have to field calls from the press all day. It pains me to say it, but I feigned more grief than was either real or necessary and made my excuses and left.

In the press office, there was a strange sense of urgency I had not witnessed before. Indeed, when I come to think about it, none of my fellow PRs had ever been remotely busy, so the scene seemed somewhat bizarre: everyone was standing up and on the phone, and no one had taken their jacket off or deposited their bags in the usual place. Each, in turn, glanced over surreptitiously, as if I'd been sent by the Head Of Forward Planning to ruin their lives.

I walked over to my desk where, unsurprisingly, my phone was ringing. I picked up the receiver. It was Derek.

'I can't believe it's true,' he said. 'My mother is sitting in the dark in the other room, and she's inconsolable.'

'I don't know what to say,' I said. 'I loved Roy and I can't believe he's dead either.'

'Roy is her life,' said Derek. 'He's all she thinks about, all she cares about. I'm worried she won't recover from this.'

Derek and I talked for a little while longer, but his desperately sad mutterings about how Roy's loss would affect his mother made me behave like one of those people with something more important to do. This is me: I could deal with real grief about as well as I could deal with the real cynicism generated by Roy's death in the meeting earlier. I felt so bad for Derek, but I couldn't speak to him with any intimacy, as the calls were now coming through thick and fast. For the record, I dealt with them one by one, assuring everyone that Roy was 'extremely happy' the last time I'd seen him, and that he'd been really looking forward to the release of his new album. Although this seemed to be the most positive response to the tragedy, I was now acutely aware that I was part of the process.

Six calls that day were easy enough to manage.

'Did I get the last interview?' each one of Roy's interviewers would ask in turn.

'Yes, you were definitely the last person to interview him,' I'd say, thus ensuring that every paper that published their interview heralded it as *Roy Orbison: The Last Interview*. The truth of the matter was that it wasn't anyone cool like Nick Kent or the *NME* that got the last interview, it was *Bella*, a women's weekly that I'd only commissioned to appeal to a broader fan base.

Mystery Girl was released on February 7 1989 and reached no.2 in the UK charts. (And that's when no.2 was really no.2.) It needed no help from me. However, there was something about knowing Roy so briefly that made me think about him again and again. It wasn't just that I had seen Roy closer to his death than Barbara had—which felt somehow unethical and wrong—it's just that I'd not even told Nick Kent what Roy had said about him.

Many years later, when I'd left Virgin and started publicizing my second Fat Les record—and yes, I admit it, I described them as *the million-selling event-led, anarchic pop art collective fronted by maverick actor/comedian Keith Allen*; and no, I can't believe they made a second record either—I was as astonished as anyone when Joe Strummer joined the throng. And yet, was it much of a surprise? Keith and Joe had been best friends for years and run Strummerville at Glastonbury as if it was their spiritual home, so when Keith asked Joe whether he'd agree to appear in a video for a new Fat Les single or turn up for a photo session for the cover of the *NME* (dressed as one of The Village People), what was he supposed to say? 'I am the lead singer of The Clash and I don't need to do anything to ruin my legacy?'

That's what he should have said, anyway.

The record in question—or should that be *the questionable record*?—was 'Naughty Christmas (Goblin In The Office)', if not the worst song of all time then surely the worst Christmas song of all time. Released in December 1998, presumably to capitalise on any good will generated by the success of 'Vindaloo', which had gone triple platinum and sold nearly a million records six months earlier, 'Naughty Christmas (Goblin In The Office)'—it's important to keep giving it its full title—captured the effervescent Christmas spirit of the office party. The video kicked off with Keith Allen changing into a green goblin outfit in the bathroom at an office party before prancing round the office 'singing' lines such as *'You naughty, naughty woman, I am naughty man'* in an inexplicable and ill-advised Indian accent. I'm assured that this is just the way goblins sing in real life, but you could hardly complain about the cast of thousands Keith had managed to rope in for the video. David Walliams, Matt Lucas, Zoe Ball, Roland Rivron, Lisa Moorish, Paul Kaye, Kieran O'Brien, Damien Hirst (OK, he was supposed to be in the band, but the footage of him getting a wad of bank notes out of a cash machine was a rather nice touch) and Joe Strummer (whirling around like he's drunk after winning the lottery) are just some of Keith's friends who now wish this episode was long forgotten. Perhaps it is—and if you're not on this list you should count yourselves lucky—but what cannot be underestimated is Keith's mission to contaminate the radio and TV airway schedules over the festive period. And no, I don't think the song has ever featured on Smooth FM's month-long transition into Smooth Xmas FM either.

Mind you, Joe did seem to be having a good time. When I first bumped into him at the Groucho on the day of the video shoot, he said, 'I know who you are Phill, but if I shake your hand it's gonna cost me £2,000 a month.' He must have been referring to the fact that this is how much I was charging for doing independent PR at the time, but it seemed a peculiar thing to say nonetheless. And then I remembered that Joe was always reinventing himself, always touring—and presumably always looking for a new PR— and he must have found out how much I cost via Keith.

'The Clash are my favourite band of all time.' I said to Joe. 'But do you know how many times you refer to cash or money in the lyrics of your songs?'

Joe looked puzzled and then intrigued.

'Twenty-seven!' I continued with a flourish, and Joe's eyes began to light up with recognition. I'd actually made the figure up, but I could easily have quoted any of the lyrics I was referring to—'*Gave all his money away*' in 'Jail Guitar Doors', '*They meant let's make a lotsa mon-ee*' in 'Complete Control', '*Turning rebellion into money*' in '(White Man) In Hammersmith Palais', '*And he loved to steal your money*' in 'Bankrobber', '*The money feels good*' in 'The Guns Of Brixton', '*I don't want to hear about what the rich are doing*' in 'Garageland', '*Just because we're in a group, you think we're stinking rich*' in 'Cheapskates', '*I needed money 'cos I had none*' in 'I Fought The Law' (actually a song written by Sonny Curtis of The Crickets, made famous by The Bobby Fuller Four, and presumably chosen by Joe due to its clever use of money terminology)—but I thought that would be labouring the point. Perhaps, in that moment, Joe realised I wasn't all about the money. But perhaps he was!

The next minute, that guy from *The Rocky Horror Picture Show*—the one who also presents *The Crystal Maze*—walks in, and Joe is all over him like some wide wide-eyed youngster who's never seen a famous person before.

'I'm a huge fan,' says Joe to Richard O'Brien, and I wonder if Joe is confusing him with someone else.

If Joe was a fan of either transvestite schlock or assault puzzling, I was not to find out, but the encounter proved one thing—Joe was enthusiastic about everything. Which explains his euphoric dance moves in the video, and the fact that he agreed to dress up as a member of The Village People for the cover of the *NME*. God knows how I persuaded the paper to do such a thing—the article suggested 'Fat Les admit they're shit' and had Alex James proclaiming 'Football and Christmas are the worst sorts of records, and obviously this is a shit record'—but a week after we'd shot the video, Keith, Alex, Damien, and Joe—and Damien's sometime manager, Jan Kennedy, who was roped in to provide that elusive fifth Village People member—were holed up in a photo studio, attempting to pull off the gayest *NME* cover shoot of all time. Naturally, they succeeded, although the sight of Joe dressed as a cowboy is something Clash fans are presumably never going to forget or forgive. Keith, of course, took it one step further and spent the night walking up and down Old Compton Street (via the Groucho) dressed as the mucho-macho leather-and-chains-clad biker from the People and camping it up with the best of them.

Two years later, I find myself promoting a Fat Les cover of 'Jerusalem', the Hubert Parry setting of the William Blake poem. The song has been chosen by Keith as a reaction to the appropriation of the hymn by far-right political groups and features the London Gay Men's Chorus and the London Community Gospel Choir, presumably as another nod to the diversity of twenty-first-century Britain. Although, as usual, there's another agenda, as Keith explains: 'The idea of great big white fascist thugs singing along with this, going, *Hang on—a choir of nonces? What's this?* That's great.' And when he says, 'This is the second time we've hijacked football for our own purposes,' you kind of know what he means.

By this point, Fat Les are a press machine. You'll read more about this later, but for the time being you should know that everyone wanted to write about them—from *The Sun* to the *NME* to *The Observer*—which was why we were at Damien's house in Devon. In 1998, *The Sun* had taken Fat Les to its heart and, for all intents and purposes, the paper's 'Bizarre' showbiz editor, Dominic Mohan (who later went on to become the editor of *The Sun*), had become part of the band—as well as the brand: I invited him to be part of the *Top Of The Pops* performance that started with Keith and his entourage on the set of *Eastenders* and followed their eight-hundred-yard chaotic passage to the *TOTP* studio set, where they pranced around (Dominic included) on stage to a largely bemused audience.* This, of course, had been part of my original plan—try

---

* This audience included all the members of The Spice Girls, who were due to perform that evening. In fact, during rehearsals earlier that day, we had bumped into The Spice Girls in the corridor waiting to go on.

'What are you lot doing here?' asked one of them. A perfectly reasonable question, considering the song was yet to be released—another PR coup—and the Fat Les entourage, twenty or thirty deep, took up most of the corridor.

Keith immediately took up the bait.

'What are we doing here?' he said, somewhat menacingly. 'I'll tell you what we're doing here. Where the fuck are you from? We're from Ing—er—land. Me and me mum and me dad and me nan, we're off to Waterloo. Me and me mum and me dad and me nan, with a bucket of vindaloo.' And then the whole of the Fat Les entourage started singing 'Vindaloo' at—and I mean at—The Spice Girls. The entourage included two of the fattest extras I'd ever seen—from The Ugly Agency—plus Matt Lucas and David Walliams (who were then only known for their Mash & Peas moniker) but I can't help thinking that the most intimidating aspect of the entire encounter was the presence of Paul Kaye, who'd humiliated the group at a recent public appearance whilst masquerading as his more infamous Dennis Pennis persona. I'd never witnessed such terror in my life.

slagging off a band in print if you're one of its members—and the ploy became so successful that *The Sun* ran several double-page spreads on 'Vindaloo'. Other quality newspapers wrote about the cultural significance of *The Vindaloo Project*, too, and by the time it was announced that Fat Les were about to release the official, FA-endorsed football anthem for Euro 2000, excitement had reached fever pitch. As I arrived at Damien's house, I'd just heard that *The Sun* was about to run an article under the headline 'YOU HAVE 31 DAYS TO LEARN THESE WORDS FOR EURO 2000'—and, below that, the words to 'Jerusalem'. And one week later? How about '10 THINGS YOU DIDN'T KNOW ABOUT WILLIAM BLAKE'? You couldn't make this up.

But the main reason we were at Damien's house was so that a photographer called Perou could shoot pictures of Keith, Alex, and Damien dressed in women's knickers, tights, and St George's Cross jumpers on one of the hills on Damien's land. The shoot was for the cover of *The Observer*'s *Life* magazine, and was to accompany Andrew Smith's interview with Fat Les, which was due to take place later that day.

The interview and shoot went without any hitches—apart from the fact that Andrew and Perou had to witness the trio's charmingly infantile antics for longer than was really necessary— but as soon as the pair had left, the drugs somehow materialised, and we all began to relax. (Or perhaps the drugs had been there all along. It was difficult to tell.) Anyway, at some point in the evening, and after I'd lost whatever inhibitions I'd brought with me down to Devon, Joe Strummer walked into the living room.

Joe lived in Taunton and was good friends with Damien, so there was nothing unusual about him turning up unannounced. He seemed more animated than ever, but I was still so unused to making small talk with the singer in my favourite punk band that our conversation must have seemed peculiarly unnatural. However, after a few drinks and a few more lines, we got talking about music, and we started to get on like long-lost friends.

At one point, long past midnight, Joe asked how I got into music, and how I ended up doing what I was doing. I could tell that he was hoping I'd reveal some deep, dark truth that I'd always loved Shakin' Stevens and I was just in it for the money, but when I told him I'd discovered music through punk and the *NME*, Stuart Henry and John Peel, he seemed genuinely interested. I mentioned that I used to have three chairs in my bedsit made out of three hundred copies of the *NME*.

And then I told him that I used to look after Roy Orbison.

'Roy Orbison!' Joe screamed, as if he was screaming, '*I hate the army and I hate the RAF.*'

'You used to look after Roy Orbison? You mean you met him? You shook his hand?' (*Will this Elvis obsession ever end?*)

'Not only did I meet him,' I said, 'but on most of the occasions we met he was wearing a white bathrobe after having come out of the shower.'

'That's incredible,' said Joe. 'Roy was the greatest singer of all time, and he's been my hero for as long as I can remember. I used to sing along to all his songs as a kid, but I never got to meet him. Tell me everything.'

So I told Joe everything I knew about Roy and about the very few occasions we'd met and how much I thought of him. And then I told him about all the interviews Roy had done for me, and that Nick Kent had bought a tape recorder for the first time so that he could get his first ever interview on tape as he loved Roy so much.

'You met Nick Kent?' said Joe. 'He's my favourite journalist of all time! I can't believe he interviewed Roy. How did they get on?'

I was beginning to suspect that the Joe sitting next to me—the one grabbing hold of my hand every now and again, and looking into my eyes as if we were brother and sister—had been sent from a lookalike agency to make me prostitute myself in front of a hidden camera and a team of TV pranksters yet to be revealed. But if it was a lookalike, it was a good one; when I asked 'Joe' about my favourite Clash songs, he had all the right answers, and the enthusiasm I'd noticed every time I met him had now reached boiling point.

I told Joe that Nick had come down from Roy's room clutching his tape recorder as if someone was about to steal it. And then I told him that after Nick left, Roy had also come downstairs and told me that it was the best interview he'd ever done.

'Roy said that Nick asked him about things he'd never been asked about before. He also told me that he wanted Nick to write his official biography.'

'Wow', said Joe. 'What did Nick say when you told him?'

'I never told him,' I said. 'Roy died before I had a chance and I just never got round to it.'

Joe's eyes lit up.

'You gotta tell him, maan!' he yelled, sounding not unlike a young Nick Kent. 'Nick has to know that Roy wanted him to write the book. How can we get hold of him?'

'I don't know,' I said. 'He married a French girl and moved to Paris.'

'We have to ring him,' said Joe, and he stood up and started leaping around the room looking for a phone directory.

Five minutes later, while I've pretended to be also looking for something reliable in book form, Joe decides to call International Directory Enquiries.

'I'd like to be connected to the Paris Exchange,' he says, and then, as if reinvigorated, 'That's amazing! Can you put me through?'

Joe managed to get through to someone, somewhere, who almost certainly lived in France and who may or may not have had connections to other people who also lived in France.

The following one-sided conversations almost certainly took place during the early hours of the morning.

'Bonjour Madame. Je suis Joe Strummer. Je cherchez pour Monsieur Kent d'habite a Paris. Vous avez any idee addresse de Monsieur Kent?'

'Non? Quelle dommage. Monsieur Kent de resides a Paris? KAY. EEE. NEN. TEE. Non?'

'Bonsoir, mademoiselle. Vous avez un certaine Monsieur Kent dans le telephonique?'

And around 5am, 'Madame! Monsieur Cunt est almost certainment un resident de Paris. Je desire un conversation avec votre superior regardez la destination du Monsieur Cunt.'

And eventually, after several more aborted attempts, 'Ou est Monsieur Cunt de la belle France? Cee. You. Enn. Tee. Non? Aarrgh!'

It was now light outside, and I'd finally persuaded Joe that he was never going to be able to find Nick Kent by shouting down the telephone at someone in France. Although I really think he gave up due to exhaustion.

A couple of years later, I was attending the 2002 *NME* Awards when I noticed that Nick Kent and Pennie Smith were due to jointly receive the 'Godlike Genius Award'. It was the first time I'd been in the same room as Nick since that time with Roy Orbison back in 1988, and it seemed like too good an opportunity to miss. But there were twenty-two awards to get through, and a lot of drinking and no eating to get through, too.

After about two hours, when all the speeches had been given and all the awards handed out, I plucked up the courage to go and find Nick's table. I stood up and wandered around the auditorium, asking anyone I knew where I'd find him, and I was shown over to a table by a wall. And there he was, holding court, with several people I didn't recognise. He seemed much older than I remembered him, but then it was an awfully long time ago.

Eventually, there was a gap in the conversation, and I leaned in and introduced myself.

'I'm Phill Savidge,' I said. 'Congratulations on your award. You may not remember me, but I introduced you to Roy Orbison in 1988, and you bought your first ever tape recorder 'cos you were such a fan. Anyway, I never told you this, but Roy thought it was the best interview he'd ever done, and he told me that I should tell you that he wanted you to write his official biography.'

Nick smiled at me like I was one of the many people that had walked over to his table that day and had the temerity to introduce themselves and congratulate him on his award. There was loud music everywhere, and I don't know if he heard anything else I said.

'Thank you,' he said politely, and then continued talking to the rest of the people on his table.

I left him to it. My work here was done.

CHAPTER 4

THE ART OF
FALLING APART

"When I was offered the PR for Smashing Pumpkins, I turned them down for the simple reason that they were American and therefore liable to fly into town demanding a press itinerary."

Punishment

I must not murder the other children in my class.
I must not murder the other children in my class.
I must not murder the other children in my class.
I must not murder the other children in my class.
I must not murder the other children in my class.
I must not murder the other children in my class.
I must not murder the other children in my class.
I must not murder the other children in my class.
I must not murder the other children in my class.
I must not murder the other children in my class.
I must not murder the other children in my class.
I must not murder the other children in my class.
I must not murder the other children in my class.
I must not murder the other children in my class.
I must not murder the other children in my class.
I must not murder the other children in my class.
I must not murder the other children in my class.
I must not murder the other children in my class.
I must not murder the other children in my class.
I must not murder the other children in my class.
I must not murder the other children in my class.

I abandoned all hope of assimilating into the comfy reaches of major record label ignominy on Friday June 1 1990. That day—or early evening, as it turned out—I walked out of the Virgin Records

THE ART OF FALLING APART

offices in Harrow Road knowing that I hated PR and that music was one of the things I used to love before life became too complicated.

I had timed my exit perfectly: England were about to take part in Italia '90 (and I couldn't see how I could enjoy this spectacle whilst having regular employment), and I had just had my first four poems published in a magazine called *The Rialto*. *The Rialto* was (and still is) the kind of magazine that recognises promise in young poets—advocates include Simon Armitage, Ted Hughes, and Carol Ann Duffy—and when I received a cheque for fifteen pounds for my efforts—the first time I had been compensated for anything I'd ever written—I knew I was going to be famous. Not *famous* famous like Sylvia Plath, but famous nonetheless.*

---

* I have been obsessed with Sylvia Plath ever since I first read her poem 'The Moon & The Yew Tree' at school, and then, in the same uncontrollable breath, when I realised that she had died in the year I was born. I began to suspect I may have retained her reincarnated spirit within my acutely poetic artifice. Subsequently, Plath kick-started—and what a suitably inapt misnomer that is—my passion for first editions, and I still have a section labelled *Plath & Related* within my library so that if it ever gets raided by ardent feminists they will see Ted Hughes in amongst its confines and believe I am on their side.

Which indeed I am.

Of course, when I stumbled upon a handwritten poem Plath had written in pencil as a teenager, together with a lock of her hair—a snip for £75,000—at an antiquarian book fair, I wondered what I would actually do if I had that kind of money. The obsession went even further when I discovered that her father, Otto Plath—such a huge inspiration for her life and work—had published a book called *Bumblebees And Their Ways*, and I started visiting rare bookstores around the country just to browse through their section on bees. I eventually found a copy at an antiquarian book fair in London; it was a large, beautiful book with, surprisingly, a bee on a budding flower on the dust jacket, and I held it for several minutes before glancing at the price and walking away. An hour later, when I went back to talk about money, the book had disappeared.

At the time, I thought it pertinent to spend my winnings on a bottle of whisky, as this is exactly what a real poet would have done after they had received independent verification of their true poetic worth.

I remember telling Sian that I wanted to leave the press office, to which she replied, 'But who's going to make me laugh?' And then she almost cried. As did I. Italia '90 and my nascent career as the greatest poet of my generation really was—once again—a big loss to the music business.

Of course, my disillusionment with Virgin really stemmed from the fact that I didn't like any of the artists I was charged with representing. John Best, my closest chum at the label, had also resigned some months earlier, and even though I had been handed his vastly superior roster (including artists like The Blue Nile and Mary Margaret O'Hara), I was still in the grip of an existential malaise that could only be lifted by the prospect of retirement. I was twenty-six years old.

On my last day, I had the usual conversations with my bands and band managers, informing them that I would speak to them the following week—obviously having no intention of doing so. I don't know why no one had been informed that I was leaving, and I don't know why I felt so awkward about telling them myself, but the truth of the matter is that on Monday June 4 1990, several people would have been put through to my extension in the press office and been genuinely shocked when they found out I'd abandoned my post. Perhaps they thought I'd been fired or had a nervous breakdown; either way, I didn't care, since I was now free to write poetry and watch the World Cup.

By this point, England were already through to the round of sixteen, and I saw them beat Belgium and Cameroon and lose to West Germany on penalties—on my tiny portable television—before a word of poetry had been written. Oh but what words! What poetry! Or perhaps not, for I have to confess that as much as I enjoyed some small success in some of the shortest-lived and even smaller-circulated poetry journals of the era, I also calculated that I was earning less than a pound a day for my endeavours. As my mathematics tutor might have said—and did indeed scribble on my final term report card—*It is now time for him to panic.*

Just as I was about to do so, the phone rang.

'Hi Phill,' said a friendly voice. 'It's John. John Best. I know you said you've retired and you only want to write poetry, but d'you fancy coming to help me out for a few days? I've just been given the Pixies and the Cocteau Twins, and I could really do with a hand.'

'OK,' I said.

John worked from his house in Camden Square and, a couple of months later, I started helping him out one day a week, until I began to realise that it was impossible to set up an interview and then disappear for an entire week before checking up on whether the interview had actually taken place or not. And *don't ring me tomorrow, ring me in a week* just sounded pathetic, so I agreed to work three days a week. And three became four, four became five, and I was soon in the midst of a life I thought I'd left behind.

Except this was somehow different. The Pixies and Cocteau Twins were two of my favourite bands, and we'd somehow chanced upon them at exactly the right moment: in August 1990 the Pixies' third album, *Bossanova*, reached no.3 in the UK charts, and 'Velouria', the first single to be lifted from the album, became their first ever Top 40 hit. The Cocteaus also enjoyed their biggest success around this time, with their sixth album, *Heaven Or Las Vegas*, reaching no.7—their highest chart position. *The Observer* retrospectively included the album in its Top 100 albums of all time, but I was more amused by the fact that this was the first time *Smash Hits* had ever contacted our 'offices': the utterly sublime 'Iceblink Luck' had become the band's second Top 40 hit, and *Smash Hits* wanted us to fax over the lyrics so they could reprint them in the magazine. There was silence on the other end of the line when I pointed out that *their guess was as good as mine* and they'd have to listen to the song and work it out for themselves.

By this juncture, we were called Best In Press and commandeering *NME*, *Melody Maker*, and *Sounds* covers on a regular basis. One week we had a band on the cover of all three, and our success soon meant we were awarded the entire 4AD roster. This included Dead Can Dance, Throwing Muses, Ultra Vivid Scene, Pale Saints, and Lush, but it was John's blossoming relationship with Lush's singer, Miki, that necessitated a move out of our makeshift offices in Camden Square to an office in Greenland Place, in the same dingy building as fashion designers Flyte-Ostell and Vivienne Westwood, deep in the heart of Camden.

In the midst of 4AD mania, we'd also taken on Liverpudlian outfit The Farm, who had the sense to immediately have a hit with 'Groovy Train'. Three months later, we'd already secured an *NME* cover—the 'When Harry Met Scally' strapline referred to the band cavorting with *Brookside*'s Harry Cross (now there's a time capsule!) on the cover—when the band released 'All Together Now', a song produced by Madness's Suggs (who managed them for a while) and inspired by the Christmas Day truce during World War I. 'All Together Now' took the band to another level, peaking at no.3 and staying in the charts for several weeks, becoming a terrace anthem of sorts. The success helped catapult the band's debut album, *Spartacus*, to the no.1 spot in March 1991, and made them something of a fixture on *Top Of The Pops*: at one point I seemed to be visiting the *TOTP* studio every other week and constantly fibbing to the *Sun* and *Star* newspapers (who'd followed us down there) about the identity of The Farm's lead singer, Peter Hooton.*

---

* God knows how they couldn't tell—he was the only one singing the whole song into the microphone on the *Top Of The Pops* set, and on—yes, you've guessed it— *Top Of The Pops* on TV itself the following day—but most of the band were staunch Liverpool FC supporters and still angry over the papers' treatment of their fans in the wake of the Hillsborough disaster. On each occasion, I offered them different members of the rhythm section, and we got away with it.

Whilst all this was going on, I'd been constantly listening to a song on a cassette I'd been sent by a band called Curve. It was noisy but tuneful, with an incredible female vocal and a really great beat, and it climaxed with a rap that had absolutely no place in indie music—but it worked. It was called 'Ten Little Girls' and was to be on an EP called *Blindfold*. I loved it, and I knew I wanted everyone else to love it as much as I did. I told John that I wanted to represent the EP, and he agreed. It was to be my first 'signing'.

Curve comprised Toni Halliday, who'd been briefly signed to a major label as the singer of pop wannabes State Of Play, and fellow State Of Play cohort and erstwhile Eurythmics bassist Dean Garcia. In 1986, State Of Play had released one underwhelming long-player called *Balancing The Scales* for Virgin Records before splitting acrimoniously and regrouping as 'credible' indie-alternatives. Curve subsequently signed to Dave Stewart's Anxious Records—a move suggested in some quarters to be part of an evil plan to infiltrate the otherwise impeccably staffed, nay impenetrably cool, alternative-rock scene.

I knew Toni and Dean's uncool background would work against their better interests, so I decided to send around thirty white labels with just the word *Curve* etched on to the centrepieces to all the influential tastemakers at *NME*, *Melody Maker*, and every music magazine I could think of. The strategy worked, as one of the recipients of the white labels—a member of The Stud Brothers—called me and said it was the best thing he'd ever heard.

He awarded the EP 'Single Of The Week' in the following week's *Melody Maker*, and the *NME* quickly followed suit. Soon, every music critic in England was eulogising over their connection to the zeitgeist and, their indie credentials intact, the duo's previous major-label affiliations were forgotten. Indeed, the ensuing subterfuge was so successful that when one music monthly magazine reporter—Stephen Dalton from *VOX* magazine—suggested that the wool had been pulled over the eyes of the discerning indie public, his lone voice seemed un-charming and peculiarly barbed against the barrage of love and affection that had risen to the surface for these much maligned individuals. What's more, the outrageous truth that Dalton had somehow uncovered merely served to make the band more intriguing: Toni and Dean were now unwilling, glamorous intruders into a defiantly unglamorous independent music scene; a scene that had spawned shoegazing, a movement characterised by guitarists supposedly gazing at their shoes in order to avoid audience eye contact—although I think we all know that rather than staring at shoes, they were actually peering at their chord progressions and effects pedals in the dark, since they couldn't play their guitars properly—and the fact that they had arrived without anyone's permission made them even more irresistible. Shortly after the band's initial press storm, Curve played a triumphant gig at Camden's Underworld and, when the band came on, they were greeted by three hundred screaming fans and around thirty journalists. I remember thinking, *This is the power of the press.*

I was on my first overseas press trip with Curve—to Boston, Massachusetts—when I first met Eurythmics' Dave Stewart. I had travelled over with Ben and Dom Stud Brother and photographer Tom Sheehan, and the plan was to bring back a *Melody Maker* cover story that would showcase Curve taking America by storm. It wasn't going to be difficult: in the early 1990s, America—for me at least—seemed to have a knack of brazenly parading conservatively attired, middle-aged, middle-class men and women in broad daylight while their black-clad younger counterparts fumed indoors, only to emerge as the sun went down. What I mean to say is that *goth will out* in the most unlikely of environments.*

I found Dave to be effortlessly sincere and enthusiastic for almost any artistic endeavour he embarked upon. Indeed, our first meeting was in a car park around the back of an unassuming venue in Boston, where he'd parked his hire car for the day, and I remember thinking that the liaison was particularly uninspiring for the pair of us.

Dave was almost as excited to meet me as he was to meet Tom Sheehan, who was sporting his customary black jeans and leather

---

* There's a place in Alaska called North Pole where it's Christmas every day and everyone's terribly happy to be, ahem, happy every day. Unfortunately, the name of the town means that thousands of letters from children from throughout the world inevitably end up in the local sorting office. The task of replying to these letters falls to the eleven and twelve-year-old children of the town's inhabitants who are confronted for the first time in their lives with the possibility that Santa does not exist. No wonder that police eventually foiled a plot by fifteen goths to kill all of the townspeople and flee to Anchorage. Yes, Anchorage.

jacket. Around his neck, Tom had hung his trusty camera. It had seen better days.

Dave was *fascinated*. He'd always wanted to be a photographer, and in recent weeks he'd finally decided to take the plunge and buy his own equipment.

'Oh what kind?' enquired Tom, with genuine interest.

'I'll show you,' said Dave, leading us over to his vehicle.

Dave opened the boot, and it was like that scene in *Repo Man* where the cop asks, 'What you got in the trunk?'—except on this occasion a cop didn't get incinerated with only his boots left for insurance purposes. Inside, I could see the finest photographic equipment known to mankind, all of which seemed to be encased in its original packaging.

'Can you tell me how this stuff works?' he asked Tom. 'I'd love to take photographs as beautiful as yours.'

'I haven't got a clue,' said Tom. 'I've never seen anything like this in my life.'

Boston was fun as it was my first grownup journey outside the UK, but it was scary nonetheless. What made it doubly fascinating was the fact that it was my first encounter with the confusion my appearance generated overseas. I'd been androgynous for quite some time—indeed, when I'd arrived at the airport, my passport had made my exit from the British Isles something of a public performance—but in the USA there was no hint of uncertainty as to my gender. I was *ma'am* to every bartender and hotel employee I encountered throughout the entire week of my stay, and what made it more amusing was that Curve's ultra-cool and equally androgynous bassist, Debbie Smith, was called *sir* the whole time we hung out in the city. We could have been girlfriend and boyfriend, although I was hardly Debbie's type.

On my first night at the hotel, I ventured downstairs and asked if I could get some room service, bearing in mind that the internal telephonic system left something to the imagination. I promise you that I was dressed in the jeans and T-shirt I'd been wearing when I'd arrived at the hotel earlier that day, but the effect was instantaneous.

'Ma'am, can I help you?' asked the man in reception.

'Yes,' I said. 'I am in room 303, but the phone doesn't seem to be working, and I'd like to get some room service.'

The man on reception glanced at the screen in front of him, the results of which presumably revealed that the inhabitant of room 303 was a Mr Savidge.

'Of course,' he said, 'that's no problem at all. But first let's just deal with your booking. We need to change this to *Mrs Savidge*, and if you could just sign this form I'll have someone come up to your room and take your order.'

The form was signed, the damage was done. And Mrs Savidge received her room service.

After our encounter in Boston, Dave and I continued to work together, masterminding Curve's stratospheric rise to prominence. To be honest, I think this was tougher on Dave than it was on me, as I think he soon discovered how owning a

THE ART OF FALLING APART

record company meant getting rid of money quickly and easily. Indeed, it was around the time of Anxious Records' formation that I first saw Dave's name in the *Sunday Times* Rich List. It said he had twenty-two million pounds. The following year there was no sign of his name.

Despite Dave's dwindling finances—don't worry, I think he's going to be OK—Curve continued to go from strength to strength, and the success of their *Blindfold*, *Frozen*, and *Cherry* EPs and debut album *Doppelganger* (which peaked at no.11) meant I was able to purloin around ten music-magazine front covers in the next twelve months. The band suddenly found themselves in the middle of several music scenes, including shoegazing—comprising bands like Ride, Moose, Slowdive, and Chapterhouse, the latter often affectionately referred to as Charterhouse by a small section of the media/PR fraternity due to the fact that they were perceived, rightly or wrongly, to be posh enough to have attended the school of that name—and *The Scene That Celebrates Itself*, a derogatory term referring to members of the burgeoning London music community who liked to hang around together, figuratively, if not demonstrably, slapping each other on the back.

By this time, John and I were looking after bands like (the already ubiquitous?) Moose, Spiritualized, Verve, and Levitation; we had moved offices, to Arlington Road, right next to a bingo hall, and taken on three people to work with us: Melissa, who was a good friend of John and Miki's; Polly, who we'd nabbed from Food Records; and Rachel, who came in from *London Student* magazine to interview Auteurs main-man Luke Haines and somehow never left.*

Naturally, with very little attention to detail, shoegazing and *The Scene That Celebrates Itself* morphed into something called *The Camden Scene*, which seemed to solely revolve around the fact

---

* Of all the artists I have represented, Luke Haines is probably the one I most admire. Sharper and more astute than your average musician, he quickly realised—after supporting Suede at their early shows and not getting the recognition he no doubt deserved—that he was destined to be a bridesmaid in all future negotiations between pop star and the public, and subsequently sidestepped the entire process by forming several bands—including The Auteurs, Baader Meinhof, and Black Box Recorder—and releasing songs and albums with titles like 'Unsolved Child Murder', 'Girl Singing In The Wreckage', 'Light Aircraft On Fire', and *After Murder Park*. With such subterfuge, he could hide his persona from the outside world and, more importantly, the prying media.

Strangely enough, Luke is the only artist to ever officially sack me: I once mentioned to him that The Auteurs were not as good as Baader Meinhof and thought he would take this on board as the preposterous comment it was supposed to be; Baader Meinhof were a side project and the Auteurs were, necessarily, the mother lode, and the fact that they were both Luke's brainchild meant that that the irony was obvious to me. (Perhaps, later on his career, when he released several records—some of them quite brilliant—under his own name, I should have suggested that Luke would never be as talented as the people behind The Auteurs and Black Box Recorder, and we could have fallen out all over again.)

Meanwhile, Luke's oversensitivity resulted in him not returning my phone calls for several days and hiring another PR company to promote his new record. I take no pride in revealing that the PR team he used failed to secure any press coverage, even though it was the same loveable old Luke that journalists and newspapers had been falling over themselves to write about for years. Towards the end of the 'campaign', I received a letter from Luke acknowledging the absurdity of the situation, and normal service was resumed.

that our offices were situated on Arlington Road.* Our roster now included The Auteurs, Pulp, Elastica, Echobelly, Menswear, The Jesus & Mary Chain, The Charlatans, and The Fall, but, prior to all this commotion, Suede somehow started the whole thing off and catapulted us into the realms of *People Who Must Be Called At All Times Of The Day And The Night.*†

---

* I first heard of Camden in the mid 1980s when I read a review of R.E.M. by Max Bell in the *NME*. I remember reading that the gig was at Camden Dingwalls and wishing that I'd been there, because I loved R.E.M. more than anything. A short while after this, I came down from Nottingham to see The Replacements at Dingwalls. They cancelled the show, so I came down to the rescheduled gig, and they cancelled that as well. The third time I came down I was standing in the queue and I recognised several people. They recognised me, and we all said, *Weren't you here for the last two shows?* From that moment on, Camden felt like a place of pilgrimage for me; when The Replacements finally showed up—on that third visit— they were more drunk than anyone I'd ever seen, but brilliant nonetheless.

† The Fall could never be described as your typical Savage & Best outfit, but the band's founder and ever-present driving force, Mark E. Smith, was worth the admission fee alone. He was the very definition of *bloody difficult*, and it is worth noting that Melissa was the only person he would speak to on a regular basis. Naturally, she was unimpressed by the confrontational and aggressive nature of his phone manner, but when Mark asked whether he could charge fees to be interviewed, I could only surmise that he hated journalists and the whole promotional process, and that he genuinely believed he was providing a valuable social service. On one occasion, when he was being interrogated by a journalist from the *NME*, in a pub round the corner from our office, he flicked the writer's rolling tobacco across the room whilst muttering, 'Loser.'

Years later, long after our paths had become uncrossed, I would bump into an inebriated version of him outside a pub during the Hay-on-Wye Literary Festival.

'Phill, is there a fucking pub round here you can smoke in?' he enquired.

'Sorry, Mark, they banned smoking in indoor public spaces years ago,' I replied.

At which point he began to swear incessantly, searching his unmanaged attire for the cigarette he'd no doubt stubbed in a pocket the minute he'd been challenged to explain his indoor smoking activities.

Suede rapidly became my favourite band, and I don't mind admitting that the very first time I heard Brett sing '*We kissed in his room to a popular tune*' I knew that I had found a lyricist I could identify with.* Several people agreed with me, and *Melody Maker*, in particular, decided that they would run a feature on the band—which actually ended up on the cover, with the byline 'The Best New Band In Britain'—before they'd even released their first single. At that first photo session—snapped by Tom Sheehan—Brett wore a cheap fur coat, and I noticed he had glitter all over his top lip. So did Steve Sutherland, who did the interview, and who finally plucked up the nerve to ask why there was glitter on Brett's face.

'Oh, a friend of mine has some glitter shorts,' Brett said. 'It gets everywhere.'

I was somewhat androgynous at the time, and it is probably true to say that Brett was the performer I would have most wanted to be: ergo, I promoted Brett with as much enthusiasm as if I was promoting myself, somehow managing to commandeer eighteen front covers before the band had released their first album. One of these—the cover of *Q* magazine—was a particular coup. Danny Kelly had recently left the *NME* to become editor at *Q*, and his way of stamping authority on the magazine was to take *NME* darlings Suede with him. Of course, Suede, weren't big enough

---

* Contrary to popular opinion, I identify with this lyric not because I am homosexual but because I admire the way Brett makes us wonder if he is kissing a boy in a boy's room or a girl in a boy's room. I thought, *Brett knows what he is doing here.*

to carry a *Q* cover at the time, since they'd only released two singles—'That Discography In Full!' was a byline in the magazine that month—and, in its own way, the cover was as big a statement as the very first *Melody Maker* cover, which had kick-started all the fuss barely a year earlier.*

A couple of months later, I became determined that *Select* should put Suede on the cover again, but the magazine was reluctant to be seen to follow in the wake of 'old man's' title *Q*. Well, how about featuring two other bands I was looking after—Pulp and The Auteurs—and putting them together with Denim and St. Etienne in a piece that encapsulated all that is great about being in a British band in 1992—and then putting Suede on the cover? Of course, a combination of circumstances meant that Brett ended up on the cover with his image superimposed on a backdrop of a Union Jack and the words 'Yanks Go Home' emblazoned alongside. Stuart Maconie, Andrew Harrison, Andrew Collins, and I had just stumbled across Britpop—although it's probably true to say that Stuart, John Robb, and Steve Lamacq simultaneously coined the term—and a movement was born.

Interestingly, I believe it was only the ever-present nature of all our artists in our Camden office—and their being interviewed in a pub called the Good Mixer, a restaurant called George & Nikki's,

---

* Incidentally, that issue of Q was the lowest-selling Q cover of its time— something I'm very proud of—but it's possible that it had been influenced by the Christmas edition of the previous year's NME, for which Brett had dressed up as Sid Vicious on the cover; the issue had proved to be the biggest-selling NME for a decade.

and another pub, the Edinburgh Castle—that lent The Camden Scene its name.* The Good Mixer, in particular, felt like our own private joke: it seemed like a very funny idea to send some of our more spoilt, coiffed *artistes* to a spit-and-sawdust pub peopled by some of the more troubled residents of Arlington House, a rest home for gentlemen afflicted with addiction to the demon drink; if they can survive this, I thought, they'll be able to survive talking to the *NME* or appearing on *Top Of The Pops*.

Around this time, I began to think I could get away with anything—even dungarees and sling-backs—and I became utterly obsessed with press, avoiding all record-company meetings and constantly diverting managerial calls to other members of the team. When I was offered the PR for Smashing Pumpkins, I turned them down for the simple reason that they were American and therefore liable to fly into town demanding a press itinerary, an interview schedule, and a management meeting where one of us was going to say *awesome* every five minutes. It seemed like far too much trouble.

On those rare occasions that I did make a record company meeting, I sat in a corner and pretended to be … enigmatic. This was easily done, as most record-company types are too vain to notice anyone else anyway, and when I was asked what kind of press I would be going for, I used to shrug and say, 'Everything.' This

---

* George & Nikki's was actually called the Golden Grill, but everyone called it George & Nikki's—except for the people that called it School Dinners, since all their food looked and tasted like the food we ate at school.

shut everyone up, since they could hardly criticise me for not being thorough. Most meetings ended in indecision anyway, and more often than not, at the last minute, some bright spark would suggest that we put the record back a week. Everyone would agree, and then we'd all shuffle back to our offices to amend our schedules.

Our own press meetings were few and far between, but we still got press—*mountains* of the stuff. We used to *weigh* it, it was so cumbersome, and, at the height of our ventures, we didn't seem to have to work particularly hard to get it.* I mean, we were good anyway—and Curve, Pixies, and Cocteau Twins were testament to the fact that we could compete with the best of them—but after the *Melody Maker* ran its Suede 'Best New Band In Britain' cover, we were deluged with enquiries, not just about Suede but about anything else we were working on.

At some point, everything we touched seemed to go crazy, and there were bands that signed enormous contracts because of their connection with us. Menswear, in particular—who I unfairly described at the time as *a post-modern experiment between a PR company and the music press*—benefited hugely from their association with us and ended up signing to London Records because the A&R guy had his hand up at the wrong moment.

---

* We actually ran a competition in *Select* magazine for readers to guess the correct weight of the Suede 'bible', i.e. all the press cuttings that Suede had had to date. The answer was 2.2kg and a winner was plucked from a hat and duly informed. I never got around to sending the winner anything due to utter crapness, and occasionally one of my colleagues—either Melissa, Polly, or Rachel—would slap the 'bible' on my desk, as if to say, *What are you going to do about this?*

It was '£200,000 ... £250,000 ... £300,000 ... £325,000 ... £350,000 ... sold to that man there!' He went, 'Argh!' and everyone laughed and left the room. Personally, I thought the band's songs had a certain charm, but they didn't really know what they were bidding for.

Events got out of hand in several other ways. I once biked over a copy of Suede's third single, 'Animal Nitrate', on a purple velvet cushion to John Mulvey at the *NME*, together with a handwritten note that said, *Another Great Disappointment*. The cushion had been lying on the sofa in our office for as long as I could remember. I never got it back, but it seemed strangely worth it, just to make a point. 'Animal Nitrate' became *NME*'s 'Single Of The Week', and the note was referred to in the paper—but perhaps not the cushion, I can't remember.

The following year, I invited *Select*'s Andrew Collins into our office to listen to 'Stay Together'—the band's first new material since *Suede*, the fastest-selling debut album since the Sex Pistols' *Never Mind The Bollocks*. We listened to the song in a sealed glass room—I even intimated that the rest of my office had not heard the track yet—and Andrew was sworn to secrecy as to the direction the band was now taking. I knew indie PR companies didn't behave like this—this was a ruse usually undertaken by major labels promoting artists like Genesis, Pink Floyd, and Queen—but I felt it was respect that a band like Suede deserved. And when Andrew left, I asked him to review the single in the magazine on its own page, with no other single reviews in sight.

Surely Andrew was in on the plan, but in this way I hoped Suede would make a statement, up there with the full-page review of 'Fool's Gold' I'd seen in the *NME* in 1989, or the five exclamation marks (rather than stars) that The Clash's *Give 'Em Enough Rope* had been awarded in *Sounds* many years earlier. Naturally, 'Stay Together' got its own full page and a glowing review.

There were several other examples of unencumbered ostentation. Every press release I wrote ran to several pages in length, and I produced a spoof price list detailing the costs involved if journalists wanted the band to discuss certain subjects or appear with members of combative bands—Elastica and Blur were obvious suspects—or photo sessions and interviews. Much later, when the band were due to release their fourth album, *Head Music*, I insisted that Brett would only do a phone interview with the *NME* to accompany their cover story. This felt like a natural progression from merely just commandeering a cover to promote a new release: perhaps, one day, Brett would only have to be recorded breaking wind and the magazine would get the story they needed. Cue frustrated protestations from a very pissed off Damon Albarn: 'Phill, how the fuck did you manage that? Why do I have to meet them and he gets away with a phoner?'

Of course, one of the consequences of me avoiding meetings and interview schedules was that we ended up only representing British acts. It wasn't as if I was anti-American; it was just that bands like Pearl Jam, Nirvana, and Soundgarden seemed to be everywhere, and when Suede came along—a band that appeared to

LUNCH WITH THE WILD FRONTIERS

be celebrating Englishness as much as anything else—I was in my element. Bands were really *dowdy* in those days—even the word *grunge* made me shudder—and released value-for-money EPs; Suede made it matter what you looked like and released fantastic singles (admittedly with colossally significant B-sides) like bands I could remember from the 1970s—T. Rex, Cockney Rebel, Roxy Music—but they also portrayed a seemingly complicated but eminently fathomable sexuality that journalists felt extremely comfortable writing about. And the fact that, initially, they were either in our office or around the corner and playing live every week didn't do them any harm, either.

In 1992, we won the *Music Week* Award for the best publicity campaign, the judges suggesting we *took Suede from obscurity to accolades to being hailed as the best band of the year.* The *Modern Review* went even further, maintaining, 'Suede's personal marketing man is reckoned to have done such a good job that the company have changed their name to Savage & Best.' It's true, we changed our name, although I can't say that John was particularly happy about the idea. (Incidentally, I should point out that I didn't want to confuse journalists with the correct spelling of my surname.)

Looking back, it's not difficult to work out why Suede received so much attention: quite simply, they changed the rules of pop music, and everyone else just followed. When they formed back in 1989, independent music was something to be sidelined, not celebrated, and bands—in fact, most of the bands we went on to represent in our early days of independence, like Moose, Curve, and Lush—released EPs and, yes, gazed at their feet. Being successful didn't come into it. Three million album sales later, with the release of *Coming Up* (an album that contained five Top 10 singles), Suede had completely redefined the left field and called it mainstream. Without them, I doubt whether bands like Oasis, Blur, and Pulp would exist in quite the same way. Indeed, whilst they may have spurned/spawned Britpop, Suede's cultural impact was of far greater significance: they represented nothing more or less than the voice of disaffected youth.

This is a fact hinted at in their unprecedented press profile over those early years. This set a PR rollercoaster in motion that meant they could legitimately feature on the cover of over sixty British magazines over the next few years—I actually signed a deal with Saul Galpern for Nude Records to pay us £500 for every front cover, a deal that Saul no doubt regretted every time he visited the newsagents—and receive the kind of plaudits usually awarded to Pulitzer Prize–winning novelists, monthly and broadsheet album reviews that regularly stretched to two pages and received full marks (though not in the *NME*, more of which later), and 'Single Of The Week/Month/Year' awards in most of the music papers. They were shortlisted for the Mercury Music Prize twice, won it once, and were one of only four 1990s artists to have an album in *The Guardian*'s '100 Best Albums Ever'. This wasn't achieved without a huge amount of hard work and meticulous attention to detail by ... well, me, actually. Indeed, when I come to think about it, I assure you that if I hadn't been at the top of my game, Brett would have taken any opportunity to sack me. Indeed, even now, I find it extremely difficult to ascertain who was more obsessed by the possibility of a front cover—him or me.

Suede's first *i-D* front cover was a case in point. When I'd originally mooted the idea of an *i-D* piece, Brett had commenced the usual *is it a cover?* routine, and I'd replied, 'Yes, but you'll have to wink like all their cover stars.'* He didn't take too kindly to this—he actually proffered 'I'm not fucking winking' as his first form of resistance—and when I related the news to *i-D* editor Avril Mair, she initially appeared unimpressed. Then, when the dust had settled and she remembered how much she loved Suede, and Brett in particular, she agreed to his demands, and we were in business. There was to be a compromise, however: Brett had to agree to be photographed with a naked 'supermodel'. And she would be winking.†

I don't know how we navigated through the subsequent *what the fuck has a naked supermodel got to do with our music?* conversations, but we did. Perhaps the fact that Avril had commissioned Jean-Baptiste Mondino—the man responsible for

---

* The wink is meant as a graphic representation of the magazine's logo.

† Interestingly enough, Suede's second *i-D* front cover, shot by Nick Knight for the September 1996 issue of the magazine, also didn't feature Brett winking. This time, we got around the golden rule with clever use of lighting; subsequently, in the weeks that followed this similarly groundbreaking cover, I used to annoy/amuse everyone in the office by rather pompously announcing (apropos of nothing), 'He will never wink, his face will only ever appear merely in shadow.'

directing the multi-award-winning video for Don Henley's 'Boys Of Summer', as well as videos for Prince (one of Brett's heroes), Madonna, and Sting—to shoot the cover persuaded Brett that it was going to be a serious affair.

The day of the shoot dawned—it was September 1994, and the release of Suede's 'difficult' second album, *Dog Man Star*, was just around the corner—and Mondino had already flown in from Paris and was now en route in a cab from Heathrow to a photo studio in London's East End. The idea was that Brett and I would meet him there, but the reality was that, when I arrived at Brett's house on Shepherds Hill in north London, no amount of knocking, banging, or shouting would rouse its inhabitants. I knew how important the shoot was to both Avril and Mondino—the latter was due to fly back to Paris later that day—so I took matters into my own hands and climbed in through a tiny bathroom window.

No sooner had I materialised in the hallway of Brett's house than he sauntered in from a side room, wearing a dressing gown.

''Allo, Phill!' he exclaimed, through what I suspected to be a fake yawn. 'Sorry, I overslept. I guess I'd better get dressed.'

It was quite obvious to me that Brett hadn't been to bed, and that all my shouting and banging had merely panicked him into an attempt to feign a proper night's sleep. I don't know who he thought he was kidding—in fact, I was vaguely insulted that he thought me gullible enough to fall for this ploy in the first place—as there were several clues to indicate my instincts were right: he smelt of alcohol and cigarettes—one was still burning in the ashtray—his pupils were like saucers, and he had dark circles under his eyes. Oh, and he was still wearing his shoes and socks from the night before.

I'm hardly Mother Teresa, so I forgave Brett immediately, but I still spent over an hour making coffee, twiddling my thumbs, and waiting for him to get his shit together. By the time we arrived at the studio in East London, we were almost three hours late. Jean-Baptiste smiled through gritted teeth, but he seemed genuinely pleased that Brett had even bothered to turn up. An hour later, after he'd been through makeup, you wouldn't have guessed Brett had been awake for—no doubt—several days; he looked like a rock star again. I still don't know how he did it.

The supermodel turned out to be Stella Tennant, who was not quite yet a supermodel. She didn't know what she was doing there, but then again neither did Brett, so they made a lovely couple. When she took her clothes off, the men were asked to leave the studio—for some reason they didn't ask me—and when she sneered and winked on cue, Brett responded by glowering magnificently. He didn't wink.

Three weeks later, the magazine materialised with the cover strapline 'The Art Of Falling Apart'. The magazine's copyeditors may have stolen the phrase from the title of Soft Cell's decadent, evocative long-player, but never has a cover line seemed more appropriately administered. If you look carefully, you can still see the deep, dark circle under Brett's right eye. He may as well have been winking.

CHAPTER 5

EVERYTHING PICTURE

"You used to be in Suede, I thought. You're beautiful and rich. You're Brett's ex girlfriend and Damon's current girlfriend. And you dress so cool most girls are going to want to be you; shit, I want to be you."

LUNCH WITH THE WILD FRONTIERS

Think: Do we want this artist?

1. What was your first thought?

2. If you're not sure, forget it.

3. Is the music exciting?

4. Have they got anything to say?

5. Are they good enough for this not to matter?

6. Any discernible personality?

7. Who's their manager?

8. Do they look good?

9. Do they want to be famous?

10. Will they make the tea/smoke roll-ups?

These ten dictums were daubed on the walls of the Savage & Best offices as part of a half-hearted PR manifesto that John and I thought up. Or, perhaps, they were thought up as a call to arms for anyone who would want to break into our offices and be stupid enough to set up their own PR company. Either way, they're as good a bunch of idiotic self-help instructions as any PR self-help manual could conjure up. And it's funny how many of the nation's favourite pop stars asked whether they could put the kettle on as soon as they'd sat in our office for a couple of minutes and pretended they hadn't read to the end of the list.

One particularly unremarkable day back in 1992, Elastica formed in our office after Justine Frischmann asked us if we thought it was a good idea for her to start a band.

You used to be in Suede, I thought. *You're beautiful and rich. You're Brett's ex girlfriend and Damon's current girlfriend. And you dress so cool most girls are going to want to be you; shit, I want to be you.*

Justine promptly went off and recruited the rest of the band, but there was a strange atmosphere around the office for the next few months: of course the band were a breath of fresh air, but their demos were hugely derivative, with shades of Wire and the Stranglers, and Justine's association with Damon only led to everyone assuming that he was having an undue influence on their work. It didn't help that Blur's new album—epitomised by the band's latest single, 'Girls And Boys'—seemed to be wearing its Wire influences on its sleeve, and, latterly, there would be rumours that a tape had been spotted in our office with the words *Blur* and *Line Up*—the title of Elastica's second single—written along the spine.*

There were further entanglements at every juncture: Damon played some keyboards on the album; Justine's best friend, Jane Oliver, worked for Savage & Best, just happened to be the live-in girlfriend of Blur guitarist Graham Coxon, and one of her 'catchphrases' (*'keys, money, and fags'*) ended up as a line in 'Line Up' and almost as the title of the band's eponymous debut album.

---

* Alex James put a cassette of 'Girls And Boys' on in our office quite soon after they'd recorded it. It sounded so like an Elastica demo that I almost jumped out of my skin when Damon started singing. Alex and I were friends at the time, and he often used to play me new Blur stuff well before release, presumably because he was inordinately proud of how good they were sounding. Most of the time I begged to differ, but this time I knew he was onto something.

When Jane first started working for us, Blur were already a success, and Suede—according to Jane and half the music business—were never going to achieve anything; but then Blur disappeared to the USA for three months, and by the time they came back, Suede were everywhere, and Blur were (almost) forgotten men. Jane couldn't quite believe it. It was all a bit *messy*.*

We sat on Elastica for as long as we could, but eventually the music press could contain themselves no longer. Polly was a huge Elastica fan and perhaps a more natural fit than I could ever be—and she went on to be the band's central PR—but in those, early, nascent, nonsensical weeks, I got a call from *Melody Maker*.

'Any chance we can do a piece on Elastica?' said a voice at the other end of the phone.

'Hmm,' I said. 'I suppose so.' I thought for a moment, before adding, 'Mind you, if you do something on them, you have to promise not to put them on the cover.'

There was a perceptible intake of breath.

'You seriously don't want us to put them on the cover?'

'No,' I repeated. I heard some shuffling, and then a muffled voice shouting across their office, 'Phill Savidge is turning down the cover for Elastica!' And then, 'OK. When can we do them?'

---

* Jane used to wear Doc Martins and scuffed jeans, and she was something of a tomboy. I was no doubt in love with her, but she went on to have two children with Jamie Hewlett (half of Gorillaz with Damon). She was also (I always thought) the original inspiration for *Tank Girl*, which was created by Hewlett and featured heavily in *Deadline* magazine; funnily enough, Blur used to be all over *Deadline*, and it was the only magazine I couldn't persuade to write anything about Suede.

Needless to say, the mind games worked: even though I'd never been offered a cover in the first place, *Melody Maker* were convinced that if they ran their cover story, I'd be annoyed, the band would be annoyed, and they'd be able to steal a march on their rivals. And how could they be wrong? *Justine used to be in Suede. She was beautiful and rich. She was Brett's ex girlfriend and Damon's current girlfriend. And she dressed so cool most girls were going to want to be her; shit,* they *wanted to be her.*

By the following year, Elastica were so successful they were competing for covers with … yes, you've guessed it, Suede. One day, we promised *Melody Maker* they could put Suede on the cover one week and then Elastica on the cover the following week. The Elastica shoot in particular was a kind of *thank you* for all the support the paper had shown since they'd thrust the band onto their cover (and into the nation's consciousness) the previous year. Everything was going according to plan until I got a call from the *NME*, insisting that they also wanted to put Elastica on the cover. I was faced with very little choice—the graduation from cover stars of *Melody Maker* to cover stars of the *New Musical Express* was no mean feat—and I had to accept the *NME*'s offer.

The trouble is that I didn't tell *Melody Maker*. Of course, I stumbled through the relevant conversations and then delayed the magazine's interview for as long as I could, but I didn't know what I was playing at: *Melody Maker* was bound to find out, and then the shit was going to hit the fan. Eventually, someone from the paper tracked me down—OK, I admit it, there were no mobile phones in those days, and I was hiding under my desk in the office—asked me why I was avoiding them, and I admitted my misdemeanour. Naturally, the editor went berserk and accused me of 'dropping my trousers' every time the *NME* wanted something—which, I had to concede, was a charming accusation. Then he put the phone down and arranged for Suede to be taken off the cover.

What drama, what japes! If the Great British Public knew that they'd been prevented from gazing upon their favourite London glam hipsters' mugs by a childish dispute between a shy but uncontrollable PR and a testosterone-fuelled editor, they would have choked on their cornflakes. Oh how we laughed! Indeed, here amongst the ruins of our professions lay the true axis of power.

But stranger things have happened. In October 1994, Menswear formed in Camden's Good Mixer pub and were on the cover of *Melody Maker* before the public had heard a note—essentially because they only had two songs, 'Daydreamer' and 'I'll Manage Somehow'. Not for the first time, Savage & Best was accused of hype, but the band suddenly became the very essence of Britpop, and everyone wanted to write about them. By the following June, *Melody Maker* had put them on the cover again—to highlight The Camden Scene—and three weeks later they ran a Britpop cover story, with Paul Lester suggesting, 'What we are seeing is the thrilling full-blown renaissance of British pop. Truly we may never have had it so good.' One month later, on August 14 1995, Oasis released 'Roll With It' and Blur released 'Country House';

two days after that, Damon presented a BBC2 Britpop special featuring Elastica, Echobelly, Menswear, Powder, and Pulp—all Savage & Best acts—as well as Blur, Boo Radleys, and Supergrass. Surprisingly, Suede and Oasis were nowhere to be seen.

By this point, we'd started dabbling with much poppier fare like Space and Dubstar, the latter produced by Stephen Hague and represented by William Rice, who very nearly didn't get the job he'd applied for. William wrote to me, addressing his correspondence to Mr Savidge, and I promptly threw his letter in a bin; John fished out the letter, and I agreed we should give him a chance. William immediately procured Dubstar an inordinate amount of press attention, and the band went on to achieve five Top 40 singles, their album, *Disgraceful*, achieving gold status in the process. Two years later, William's campaign for Texas's six-time platinum album *White On Blonde* would win the *Music Week* PR Award, and I knew I'd met more than my match.

We'd also branched out into dance music with the hiring of dance PR Addi Merrill—we later moved on to represent Faithless and Erasure—and started our own record label, Parkway Records.* I'd actually wanted to call the label No Records so I could answer the phone and shout 'No!' when people rang the office. Unfortunately, John said no. The label was our way of saying

---

* Addi seemed to know everything there was to know about dance music and nothing about indie or popular music at all. Once, when David Bowie's 'Life On Mars' came on the radio in the office, she said, 'Who's this?' I picked up all my bits of work related material off my desk, placed them in my bag, walked out of the office, and went home. When I left, Polly said, 'You've done it now, Addi.'

everybody else is doing it so why can't we?, but our first two signings felt like a veiled attempt to second-guess the mores of the indie buying public. The first of these, Powder, featuring Pearl Lowe on vocals, sold 1,500 copies of their debut single, '20th Century Gods', in the first two days of its release and topped the indie charts, but it was all downhill from there. The second, the all-girl faux-punk outfit Fluffy, always felt part of an ever decreasing circle of a talent/achievement hybrid: if Suede were Suede—and I think we can agree that they were—then Elastica were a female Suede, Menswear were a male Elastica, and Fluffy were a female Menswear. So what would a male Fluffy look and sound like? I dreaded to think.

Strangely enough, what chiefly attracted me to Fluffy was not their louche demeanour and provocatively displaced attire but instead the prospect that representing them might be a lot of fun. At one point, when John suggested they were a 'throwaway' act, I yelped, 'If Hall Or Nothing can have their Shampoo, then I want my Fluffy,' referring to our friendly PR rivals, Hall Or Nothing, who were no doubt enjoying themselves looking after British girl duo Shampoo and their recent hit single 'Trouble'.

In their earliest incarnation, Fluffy boasted a bass player named (magnificently, I thought) Pandora Ormsby-Gore, who opened up a whole new set of PR opportunities. The band released 'Hypersonic' (which featured an image of a dildo on the sleeve) and 'Husband' (which didn't), but the band were constantly in the spotlight due to our own, somewhat inappropriate public profile.

Every newspaper that wrote about them referred to Savage & Best in the headline—'Put that in your hype' (*The Guardian*)—or mentioned a 'media masterplan' in the article; Dave Stewart signed them to Anxious Publishing, presuming our involvement to mean they were the *next big thing*; and ex-Geffen A&R man Tom Zutaut (famed for signing Guns N' Roses) flew over to meet John and me—and the band's manager, Phil Hope—with a view to signing the band to The Enclave, his newly created imprint of EMI. Even 'superstar DJ' Pete Tong contacted us on a daily basis asking if he could release their music through London Records.

But we must have done something right, because Fluffy appeared on the 1996 *NME* Bratbus tour (with The Cardigans, The Bluetones, and Heavy Stereo), and I managed to get out to Miami and New Orleans—the latter for a Floria Sigismondi video shoot—before anyone noticed that the band weren't selling any records. We got out just at the right time: ex-Clash/Sex Pistols engineer Bill Price was producing the band's debut album at Metropolis Studios, and costs were escalating; The Enclave had now signed the band to a two-album deal, and the 'piece of the action' we were promised seemed to involve us being culpable for several hundred thousand pounds of recording costs and tour support. Eventually, The Enclave folded and Fluffy split, and no doubt I breathed a small sigh of relief.

If Fluffy taught me one thing, it was that as long as our name was attached to an artist, we could guarantee them unlimited press exposure. I took this to mean that we could represent a band I disliked—as long as I didn't have to look after them myself—on the understanding that I knew they'd be successful. This explains the presence of Kula Shaker on our roster.

Kula Shaker were fronted by the handsome, debonair figure of Crispian Mills, the grandson of legendary actor Sir John Mills and son of actress Hayley Mills and film director Roy Boulting, and, after jointly winning—with Placebo—the 1995 *In The City* contest and promptly signing to Columbia Records, I reckoned they were a dead cert for mainstream success. Indeed, with such exalted heritage and a major-label budget behind them, what was not to like? Well, the band's music for a start, which I always found contrived and derivative in equal measure. Melissa agreed to represent them, and I knew she'd do a terrific job, so I let her get on with it.

There's no accounting for taste, of course, and Kula Shaker proved to be a great success, their debut album, *K*, becoming the fastest-selling debut album since … *Elastica*. The album went on to sell 850,000 copies in the UK alone—we were getting good at this predicting lark—but it felt like I'd started my own version of Reggie Perrin's *Grot* shops.* I was having much more fun making

---

* I first started predicting chart positions during the Top 40 countdown with my sister in the 70s. Then, at the end of that decade, I heard Tubeway Army's 'Are "Friends" Electric?' on the radio before it came out and I knew it would go to no.1. By the time Savage & Best was in its stride, I was so good at guessing chart positions that I correctly predicted all JJ72's final single and album chart placements from their midweek spots. JJ72 were signed to Lakota (via Sony) at the time, and the label's boss, Conor O'Flaherty, started to believe I was some kind of sage. On August 25 2001, when Conor picked me up from my Dublin hotel so he could drive me to

up my own versions of their songs; '*I won't do Vogue but I will do Tatler*,' I used to sing along (in my best posh-gone-cockney twang) to the chorus of 'Tatva', their no.4 smash hit.

In July 1996, Kula Shaker played the T In The Park festival, but I managed to miss them due to the effects of a terrible hangover induced by the events of the day before. *That* day I'd been dressed as an androgynous alien all day—I was wearing a pair of silver mirrored trousers that blinded everyone when I walked in their vicinity—but if my Second Proper Girlfriend was put out by my appearance, she never said anything: I often wore dungarees and women's suits and trousers, hoping that these would enhance my feminine look.*

After seeing Beck (who my Second Proper Girlfriend represented at the time), we left the festival so that we could check into our hotel before the hordes arrived. My birthday was the following day, and we were in an ebullient mood when we arrived at the

---

Slane Castle, where the band were supporting U2, we passed a small club, and I noticed a beautiful goth woman entering its premises.

'What's that place called?' I said to Conor, pointing in the direction of the club. Conor looked at me as if he had stumbled upon the new Messiah.

'I don't believe it,' he said. 'You've only gone and done it again. That is the very same club where JJ72 played their first gig.' He shook his head. 'Phill, you're amazing,' he added.

I didn't have the heart to tell him I only wanted to know the name of the club as it seemed like a nice place to meet beautiful goth women.

* In the office I would often got mistaken for one of the women who worked for Savage & Best, and couriers or dispatch riders would always bring parcels over to me after asking for Melissa, Polly, or Rachel; I lost count of the times that managers and record company executives arrived looking for 'Phill Savidge' only to leave after several minutes, presuming me to be John's PA.

hotel after listening to Underworld's 'Born Slippy' on full volume for what-seemed-like an eternity; never had the words '*mega mega white thing*' seemed so pointless and so poignant at the same time.

At the hotel reception, we gave our names and were told that our room was the largest and best room in the hotel. My Second Proper Girlfriend and I exchanged a look that said *I knew you were planning something special* and, after we dismissed the need for help with our bags, we were handed our key and told to make our way to the top floor. We took the lift and emerged on to the top floor of the hotel, still laughing at the absurd reflections my trousers made in every mirror we passed. Then we put the key in the door.

'Wow,' I said, my eyes darting around the room. 'This is the biggest room I've ever seen. Look, there's two bathrooms and about four bedrooms!'

My Second Proper Girlfriend walked over to one of the doors in the far corner of the room and opened it.

'Look,' she said. 'There's even a kitchen.'

'And champagne!' I said, reaching inside the fridge.

I fetched two glasses, opened the bottle, and poured two glasses of champagne. We clinked our glasses, hugged each other, and went to sit on one of the sofas dotted around the main living space.

'What a great birthday surprise,' I said once we were sitting down. 'How did you manage to pull this off? Beck?' I added, referring to my Second Proper Girlfriend's connection to the multifarious American singer songwriter.

'What d'you mean?' she replied. 'I thought you'd organised this?'

'No,' I said. 'It's nothing to do with me.'

I glanced around the room again, and it was only then that I noticed several flight cases propped up against a wall.

'This isn't our room,' I said in a mild panic. 'Look at all those flight cases.'

'What's that on the table?' said my Second Proper Girlfriend, pointing at a large white block sitting on the glass-topped table in front of us. I half stood up, reaching over to see what she was talking about.

'It's a massive block of coke,' I said in astonishment, picking it up with both hands. 'This is ounces of the stuff.'

I sniffed the block and, having confirmed that it was what I thought it was, placed it back on the table. Then I walked over to the flight-cases to see if any of them were tagged with ownership details. They weren't.

'What are we gonna do?' said my Second Proper Girlfriend. 'This isn't our room.'

I started walking round the room, glancing at various rucksacks and suitcases sitting on chairs and stuffed under desks. I didn't want to open any of them, since the last thing we needed was to be caught rifling through someone's belongings when they got back to their room. Then I saw an A5-sized black booklet placed under a lamp on the corner of a desk. I knew what it was instantly and picked it up to check the contents.

Tour Itinerary, it said on the cover.

'This room belongs to *Insert Band Name Here*,' I said.* 'Or it's their crew's room, at any rate. This is their itinerary.'

'Shit,' said my Second Proper Girlfriend, standing up immediately. 'What if they come back and find us here?'

'I don't think they will,' I said, leafing through the contents of the book in my hands. 'It says here they're on stage in about half an hour, and there's no way they're gonna come back here before then.'

My Second Proper Girlfriend sat down again, and I sat down next to her on the sofa. We both stared at the enormous block of coke on the glass-topped table in front of us. Then we both looked at each other.

'D'you think they'd notice?' I think we said in unison, and before either of us could think up a counter argument, I fetched a small knife from the kitchen and started to carve a small chunk off the edge of the block. Then I smashed the chunk up and chopped it into several lines before snorting one of them up with flamboyant abandon. My Second Proper Girlfriend followed suit,

---

* Incidentally, you will notice that I am being curiously evasive about the identity of the band whose room we were in. This isn't because I can't remember who they were, but simply because I am wondering if the band in question might contain members who are considering going into politics and would be compromised by my revelation that they had a ridiculous amount of cocaine in their hotel room— even if this was during a particularly hedonistic period of the 1990s. Naturally, this has become much more likely since Blur's drummer Dave Rowntree stood for the Labour council in the City of Westminster in 2007—although I'm not suggesting for one minute that Dave has ever been anywhere near a hotel where suspicious substances were located. However, I wonder if I'd be better off suggesting that all we'd found were some yoga mats and herbal teabags? Perhaps that'd be even more litigious? You can see my predicament.

and we spent several minutes laughing and discussing our stroke of good fortune. An hour later, after consuming all of the lines we had set out in front of us, the effects of the coke started to become more pronounced—neither of us could see or speak properly—and we decided to vacate the room. I sliced off another chunk from the block before pocketing it and closing the door behind us with a sigh. Then we ventured downstairs to return the room key, leaving it on the front desk when I noticed the receptionist become distracted.

We kept a low profile around the hotel for the rest of the weekend, after finally plucking up the courage to ask another receptionist whether we could have the key to our room. This time she gave us the correct key to a much smaller room with a lot less coke in it.

The following year, Kula Shaker played T In The Park again, but I was five hundred yards away from their stage, walking past with my hands over my ears, shouting, 'I shall never see them.' By this point, my Second Proper Girlfriend and I were on rocky ground, and it proved to be the last festival we attended together. Naturally, I would progress to a state of misery for several months, but I soon contented myself with the fact that I had stumbled across a band I believed to be the future of rock'n'roll. Later, I would go on to describe Ultrasound as *the very definition of Britpop excess*, but for the time being they were like nothing else I'd ever seen in my life.

I first heard about Ultrasound when several *NME* journalists—

and Nude's Saul Galpern—kept calling me and suggesting that I had to see them live at the earliest opportunity. I read an *NME* review of their debut single, 'Same Band', which described it as 'sounding like The Who's *Tommy*—in its entirety—squeezed into four-and-a-half minutes … utterly heroic and bizarrely, by some distance, their most understated moment', and I knew I had to see them. I was not in the least bit prepared.

Ultrasound seemed to inhabit some netherworld halfway between Grand Funk Railroad, early Hawkwind, and just about every progressive rock, punk, and glam group—punk Floyd, anyone?—you'd known and loved from around 1970 onwards. Their songs were gloriously epic in proportion, but it was really their line-up that took your breath away: drummer Andy Peace and keyboard player Matt Jones were utterly unaffected, flawless musicians; bassist Vanessa always seemed vaguely pissed off (which is how I like my pop stars to look) but was mesmerising nonetheless; and Richard, their guitarist, looked and played like a Bernard Butler in waiting. Nothing, however, prepared you for the presence of their singer, Tiny, who was anything but, a man housed—I use the term advisedly—in velour who had the most cracked up, delicately nuanced voice I'd ever heard. I don't know if I mentioned he was the wrong side of twenty stone.

I had never fallen in love with a band whose lead singer was so hefty, and it took some getting used to. And it wasn't as if Tiny tried to hide his hugeness on stage, either: every time there was a break in one of the songs towards the end of the set, Tiny would start fiddling with his velour top, and I could sense the enormous folds of fat about to discharge themselves over the top of his trousers. It was a too-afraid-to-look moment, and when I finally started to represent them, I used to glance around the audience, just to check whether any of the journalists I had invited had noticed what I'd noticed. Of course they had, but I had to make sure.

Tiny presented me with a conundrum: I was used to wanting to be or to look like the lead singer of my favourite rock band, but with Tiny I didn't want to do either of these things. It was almost as if they had bypassed all of my usual reference points and gone straight to the heart of the matter: I took their songs home with me and danced around in a state of euphoria in front of a full-length mirror singing '*Sometimes when it rains I see a rainbow*' ('Floodlit World'), '*Gary Glitter's gone to seed so who will lead us now?*' ('Stay Young'), and '*I once was young and full of fire / But life is cruel and I am kind*' ('Suckle'), but I still couldn't see how I was supposed to relate to their singer. And yet I was transported to a world where none of my prejudices mattered.

I wasn't alone in my predilection for all things Tiny. The band signed to Nude Records, and the music papers fell over each other to write about him. No doubt he proved a divisive figure in editorial meetings—perhaps editors and publishers were heard to discuss the particular merits of black music, heavy metal, and now fat people as devices for selling (or not selling) magazines to white, indie audiences—but they stuck to their guns nonetheless: Tiny was on the cover of a June 1998 *NME* (shot by David Titlow) dressed as a king (complete with crown and sceptre), but the photo session was mainly notable for the fact that Tiny fell through the sofa in the studio but continued to act as if it was the most normal thing in the world—even though the sofa had now been rendered completely useless.*

While all this was going on, I was having an ongoing, perhaps unhealthy dialogue with Nude boss Saul Galpern about the philosophical aspects of signing a band who were so far outside of the mainstream, you had to create a whole new genre just to describe them. Saul had fought off every major record company in order to sign the band, but I tried to convince him—in an attempt to amuse myself—that the music industry had been planning to destroy him for years; Ultrasound was their way of getting him back for making Suede so successful.

When Saul and I commissioned the band's first official photo session, I would ring him and ask if we could go through the photos together so that we could pick the best shots for promotion purposes. 'Saul,' I'd say. 'Have you got the pictures in front of you now? OK, you see the one with Andy on the left and Matt on the right? And see where Richard is? Well, can you see Vanessa and Tiny in the middle? Great!' Then I'd dissolve into a bout of false

---

* Tiny actually fell through the sofa in our office, too, and didn't bat an eyelid. Perhaps he did this on a regular basis and was getting used to it by now. However, when Tiny sat in the passenger seat of my car one day and broke the axle, I had to say something. 'Tiny,' I said. 'For fuck's sake.' He looked at me for a while until I finally climbed out of the car and placed a *Broken Down* notice on the windscreen.

hysterics before proclaiming, 'I can't believe you signed them, you fucking idiot. They look like a bunch of freaks!' At this point, Saul would start to laugh, and I'd try to break the tension by suggesting I was kidding and he had signed the best band in the world, after all: naturally, I'd then move onto the next picture and repeat the whole process, so that Saul didn't know what to think; eventually, when I knew he couldn't take any more, I would confirm that, yes, they were definitely the best band in the world.

Ultrasound were moderately successful—they had two Top 40 singles—but became victims of their own and the industry's excess. When I told Tiny he could order anything he wanted for a photo session, he decided on two peregrine falcons; the birds came with trainers who explained to me that they had never been hired together as a pair due to their intense dislike for each other; the resultant photo shoot was disastrous, with most band members appearing to cower as if braced against some terrible, unseen attacker. Meanwhile, Tiny was covered in feathers.

The recording of the band's debut album, *Everything Picture*, also proved to be traumatic. The band fell out with several producers—including Radiohead producer Nigel Godrich, who lasted three days (yet still pulled the brilliant 'Aire & Calder' out of the bag), and Supergrass producer Sam Williams, who lasted ten days—and ended up producing much of the album themselves. This stint included a hastily arranged Christmas Day recording session when the band realised the album's delivery date was otherwise unachievable. When the band finally handed in the master tapes, Saul reminded them that he still had no artwork, so they decided to spend the night in our office—with countless cans of ale and several tins of paint and giant canvases—producing the artwork themselves. The result was a frightening mishmash of misshapes and mishaps that you'd be forgiven for thinking had been created in the middle of the night by five disparate souls under the influence of alcohol and cannabis.

Ultrasound released their magnum opus, *Everything Picture*—a double album that the band initially wanted to release as a triple—on April 19 1999. The album clawed its way to no.23 in the charts, although it was generally received badly, and the band never fully recovered. Nude Records promptly abseiled into financial difficulties—a situation no doubt enhanced by the album's overindulgence, budget-wise. Our office survived its paint adventures, although Savage & Best itself did not; Ultrasound would perhaps prove to be the last guffaw of the damned, as less than six weeks later, John and I agreed to go our separate ways.

CHAPTER 6

A FEW
PLAIN
TRUTHS

"I should confess that it's entirely possible that I was partly responsible for the fact that the original line-up of Suede split in 1994."

I should confess that it's entirely possible that I was partly responsible for the fact that the original line-up of Suede split in 1994. Of course, trouble had been brewing for some time, and you'll read elsewhere about how guitarist Bernard Butler felt that Ed Buller's production for the band's second album, *Dog Man Star*, was not up to scratch and thought he could do a better job himself. Butler was also beginning to find Anderson's increasing drug use problematic, and he had already started to separate himself from the rest of the band by arriving at the studio alone and putting down his guitar parts when he knew none of them would be present.

One day, Butler would return to the studio to find his guitars left outside in the corridor. To be fair, the band might have left his guitars in the corridor to protect their strings, since the studio was uncommonly warm, but Bernard had other ideas: he concluded that his services were no longer required and promptly quit the band. It's hard to fathom now, but the fallout from his 'dismissal' was a small rock'n'roll earthquake: 'Is It All Over For The Best New Band In Britain' was the kind of headline I was trying to head off at the pass—unsuccessfully, as it turned out—and still the war of words continued. The band's mainstays, Brett, Mat, and Simon, tried to show a united front, but it was Butler who triumphed with a simply put one-liner, 'I'm not mad and I am happy.' Clever. Never had I thought it more appropriate to respond, 'I'll get you, Butler,' but I remained silent. Which is very difficult when you are meant to be doing PR for a band.

Eventually, Butler was replaced by a seventeen-year-old

guitarist from Poole in Dorset called Richard Oakes. I put out a statement that Oakes had answered an ad in the music press—just like Butler—trying to create the impression that it was business as usual and seventeen-year-old guitarists always replaced twenty-three-year-olds as part of the natural order of events. Oakes was a fan of the largely forgotten progressive-rock outfit Caravan, and I spent much of my time trying to prevent him talking about them in interviews. I spent the rest of my time warding off a journalist from the *Bournemouth Echo* who seemed to be obsessed with the thought of one of their local brethren—and one who was barely more than a child—being thrust into the clutches of a bunch of decadent London reprobates.

Oakes's first public appearance with Suede was at the *Top Of The Pops* studio—now there's a baptism of fire—where he mimed the guitar parts to a song called 'We Are The Pigs'.[*] For my part, I was busy trying to keep the music papers guessing the name of the new album by faxing its title one letter at a time[†] and penning the following words:

---

[*] I always thought it was a terrible idea to release a song called 'We Are The Pigs' as your first single after half of your songwriting partnership has just upped sticks. I mentioned this to Brett on several occasions, and it was a constant source of irritation to Nude Records boss Saul Galpern at the time. My thinking was that most young people wouldn't go into a record shop and ask for something that basically says, *I am a pig*. Of course it is not as simple as that, but the single was not a great success. I rest my case.

[†] Incidentally, some years later, the band decided to reveal the title of the band's new album—*Head Music*—to Galpern and the music press one letter at a time. Now, I'm not saying that they got this from me ... but they got this from me.

There's nothing to discuss. A few plain truths. Some claims which cannot be dismissed. Let's feed the enemy. SUEDE are the best band in the entire world. They are because they are, because they know they are and (less important this) because you know they are. Their new album DOG MAN STAR is possibly the best album you will ever hear. 'Possibly' because you never know what they'll come up with next. It's early days. The heart quickens. This shouldn't be about pretending anyway. Suede don't pretend to be anything other than who they are (how redundant those early Smiths comparisons seem now) so why should we try to pretend? Suede are out there, alone and unassailable, a ship on the distant horizon. You call and you swim. A foghorn bellows its indifference. You drown.

When I read these words now, I am struck by how much I used to love this record. The style was admittedly sententious—and someone told me that Danny Baker had found my freshly penned biography so pompous that he'd actually read out the whole thing on his London radio show with Wagner's 'Ride Of The Valkyries' playing behind it—but I was merely doing what we all do when we want to be heard: we overemphasise a point to make a point. Naturally, I embarked upon the press campaign for the record with a newfound arrogance, ensuring that the record would be heard on its merits and not for the circus that had developed around it. Reviews had to be full marks or I had not done my job properly, and I got very little sleep throughout this period. Indeed, I remember the writer John Harris and I spending two very drink-fuelled evenings at my house in North London, playing a *Dog Man Star* promo in a seemingly endless loop.

'It's a *ten out of ten*, isn't it, John?' I'd say, putting the record back on again and referring to the fact that Harris was due to be reviewing the album for the following week's *New Musical Express*.

'Of course it is,' John would say, and I'd relax for at least the duration of the first half of the record. Then the debate would begin again: Can a record be perfect? Was there anything on the record that could be improved upon? At what point in the recordings did Bernard actually walk out, and how much of the record was therefore a repair job?* What other records had ever achieved ten-out-of-ten status? We couldn't think of any.†

I couldn't help thinking that John was leading me on, and when push came to shove and he was about to put pen to paper he just wouldn't be physically capable of giving the record the mark it deserved. I told him so.

'Whatever you're saying now,' I brokered, somewhat ungraciously, 'won't mean anything when you take your review

---

* This is still a debating point to this day, since when Bernard left the recordings, Brett had only recorded guide vocals and several songs were unfinished, guitar-wise, and one—'The Power'—didn't feature Bernard at all.
† In June 1997, the *New Musical Express* awarded Spiritualized's *Ladies And Gentlemen We Are Floating In Space* 9.99 (recurring), calling it 'a seismic tour de force'. Even though Savage & Best represented the record, I was strangely unmoved by the lack of a full house.

in. You haven't got the guts to stand behind your convictions. One snide comment from Steve and you'll crumble.' Steve was Steve Sutherland, the current editor of the paper and a hard nut to crack, being both a Suede fan and a hard-nosed cynic in equal measure.

'Don't worry,' John said. 'I promise you it's the best record I've ever heard, and I love it.'

Later that night, John disappeared into the cab that would take him home. I slept soundly for the first time in months. Just over a week later, I opened up the paper in eager anticipation. *Nine out of ten.* My heart sank. I'd failed. The greatest record to surface in the modern era—and I really thought so at the time—would remain unacknowledged.

I dialled John's extension at the *NME.*

'What happened?' I said, 'I can't believe it?'

'I couldn't do it,' said John. 'I just couldn't do it. No matter how good a record is, it just can't be a ten.'

I didn't say anything.

For the record, this is the best review of *Dog Man Star* that appeared at the time:

> *In April this year, Suede went back into Master Rock Studios to begin recording their second album with producer Ed Buller. The results, completed in July, have become twelve songs known as DOG MAN STAR. To call this a better record in every way than SUEDE would be an understatement of*

litigious proportions. The LP (a double on vinyl) is an hour long and begins with one of the most extraordinary songs you will ever hear: INTRODUCING THE BAND sounds like Sgt. Pepper might if it was recorded in the year 2000, Brett intoning in apocalyptic mantra 'Dog man star took a suck on a pill / And stabbed a cerebellum with a curious quill / Europe, America, Winterland / Introducing the band.' In the light of recent events (more of which later) this has to go down as one of the strongest and more healthily ironic ways to begin a record in years. The line 'I want the style of a woman, the kiss of a man' is likely to draw all the usual attention too. Later in THE WILD ONES (which Brett has called 'the best Suede song so far') and with an outro that makes the Smiths 'There Is A Light' pale into insignificance, there is a moment of pure pathos, the line 'oh, if you stay' sung mournfully against a backdrop of mellifluous violins. It is enough to make you weak.

It seems churlish once you've heard all of DOG MAN STAR to single out anything for particular praise but we shall try, we shall try; THE POWER, again over a melee of violins, might rank one day as one of those classic, tireless, wireless songs you're wont to sing in the bath ('Starman', anything by the Eagles—don't let that put you off) when you think you could rule the world from the waves you create, and like all the best songs it is really two songs rolled into one, the final 'la la la's' slipping into the distance; DADDY'S SPEEDING with echoes of Sgt. Pepper again, where Brett sends himself back in time to save James Dean crashing his car and only ends up taking drugs with him and encouraging him to do it; the rocker NEW GENERATION which appears to be so good it has two different choruses, one sung after the other and the latter the fantastically drug-addled 'We take the pills to find each other'; the ten-minute THE ASPHALT WORLD which will genuinely blow your mind with better guitar parts than STAY TOGETHER (now that's saying something) and the hippest lyrics imaginable; and finally the LP's closer, STILL LIFE, which features a forty-piece string orchestra arranged by Brian Gascoigne, best known for his work with Scott Walker— epic, does that say enough? Well, we tried, we tried.

And now the silence.

It was towards the end of the recording and mixing of DOG MAN STAR that Suede parted company with their guitarist, Bernard Butler, and it would hardly be apt to discuss why and wherefore. Butler's guitar is all over the LP, but then so are the rest of Suede, including violins and an orchestra. The Anderson/Butler partnership might be at an end, but at its apex stands DOG MAN STAR. For the record, the song THE POWER does not feature Butler, this rather revealing thought boding well for the future. Suede have now recruited a new guitarist, a seventeen-year-old called Richard Oakes from Poole in Dorset who the world should be very excited about. The future, it would seem, is in safe hands.

Very young hands to be sure, but safe hands nonetheless. And, significantly, like Butler, Richard Oakes replied to an advert in the music press.

Suede release DOG MAN STAR on October 10th. Apart from being easily the best album of the decade so far, its release is likely to change a few things, not least the state of pop music today. It is not easy to think of a better record, it is not easy to judge it against anything else. It is not a competition and if it was, it isn't any more. DOG MAN STAR will blow your head off every time you listen to it. That old adage 'the best band since The Smiths' has suddenly been eclipsed and we can rest.

The body of work is enormed.

Now, those of you who are paying attention will immediately recognise the style of these words and realise that I wrote this 'review' as part of the aforementioned biography that appeared at the time. I even wrote to the Oxford English Dictionary to ask if they would consider adding the word *enormed*—as in *made enormous*—to their lexicon. I never heard back.

In hindsight, it's easy to see why Brett picked an unknown seventeen-year-old guitarist to replace one of the best guitarists of his generation: chutzpah. What better way to confound the critics—who were suggesting that Suede were finished—than to pluck a child from obscurity (one without a track record) and to hail him as a prodigy before anyone had a chance to hear him? Of course, I knew how much the split meant to Brett: one Sunday morning, earlier that year, I'd had a call from Brett asking if I could get hold of some weed and bring it round to his house. Brett lived in the ground-floor section of a gothic mansion in Highgate, and I lived around the corner. I told him I'd be round in less than an hour, but when I arrived the scene could no doubt be described by Sky News as 'one of devastation'; there were countless vodka bottles and the usual drug paraphernalia all over the living room, and the smell of stale perfume was quite overpowering. Brett and his best friend and flatmate, Alan, were lying on a sofa looking completely wasted.

'I brought you the weed,' I said. 'It belongs to my girlfriend but you can have it. What have you been up to?' I gestured at the remains of nothing in particular.

'We took some Es,' said Alan, with some difficulty.

'And then we took some more Es,' said Brett.

'How many?' I asked.

'About fifty,' said Alan, giggling. 'But we're all tripped out and now we need to sleep.'

I walked over to the grand piano that was in the centre of the room. There was a piece of paper on top of it, and I could make out the words *great party guys!* and two names with several kisses scrawled underneath. I took out the weed and left it on the piano. There didn't seem to be much point in hanging around, seeing as I was completely straight and Brett and Alan were beyond repair. I made for the door. To my surprise, Brett managed to pick himself up from the sofa and follow me to the door.

'Everything's going to be all right, isn't it, Phill?' he said, and for a moment I wondered what he was talking about. Then I realised he must be referring to the fact that Bernard had just walked out of the band, and that his childhood dream of rock stardom was about to be sabotaged. I noticed a wizened, almost frightened look on his face that I had never seen before.*

'Of course it is,' I said, not knowing whether to believe it myself.

Naturally, Bernard was the reason why Brett could afford to get wasted in the first place. Organised and streamlined into activities that meant he always made the right decisions at the right time, in many ways he could be said to be the complete antithesis of Brett. Now, of course, without his alter ego at his side, Brett couldn't afford to lose himself in drugs—he'd have to work twice as hard to promote the new record.

But I digress: the reason that Bernard picked up his guitars and left Suede is not because he couldn't stomach Brett's drug taking, or Ed Buller's production techniques, or, indeed, the rest of the band's unwillingness to have *Dog Man Star* mixed by another party. It's because he couldn't handle Brett getting all

---

* Perhaps this is not entirely true. I had seen that look once before, when Oasis emerged with their first single and the music press went mad. For the first time since the 'Best New Band In Britain' cover, Brett felt seriously threatened by a competitor. 'They're all right,' he'd offer disingenuously, 'if you like that sort of thing.' And then, as if the thought was truly too terrible to contemplate, 'D'you think they'll cross over?' I used to reassure Brett that I very much doubted that, and he'd shuffle off, sniffing his indifference. Indeed, it was no doubt around this time that Brett's sniffing became pandemic: it was almost as if Oasis were getting up his nostrils.

the adulation for a Suede repertoire that was at least 50 percent his doing. And who could blame him? And who was responsible for Brett receiving more adulation than Bernard? Well, I suppose, I was.

* * *

The media's obsession with Suede, and Brett in particular, is well documented, but there are two incidents that both occurred in 1992 that leap to mind when I'm thinking about why Bernard left Suede. The first was at a photo session for *The Face*, which some zeitgeist aficionados had now taken to calling a 'style bible'. The band's first front cover was barely dry off the press, and there was still some confusion as to who or what Suede actually were. *The Face*, however, was utterly convinced that it knew exactly who Suede were and promptly commissioned a six-page feature to coincide with the band's second single. I communicated the news to the band and the record company and arranged for the photo session to take place.

When I arrived at the photo session in Soho, I knew something was not quite right. There was no studio as such, just someone's flat in a particularly seedy part of the neighbourhood. There were remnants of yesterday's takeaway dinner quite visible in the tatty kitchen that led away from the room we were supposed to be working in, and unless I was much mistaken I could hear the sounds of several people having sex in a bedroom at the end of the corridor. Quite apart from this, I noticed that the clothes rail that had been delicately placed at the rear of the threadbare sofa contained fur coats, sequined tops, and feather boas. At the base of the rail I noticed a selection of platform shoes.

'What's all this?' I said, pointing at the shoes and the clothes.

'Oh, you know,' came the strangulated reply from the photographer. 'They're for dressing up in. It's going to be fabulous.'

The photographer was clearly not English and had no doubt been flown in for the day to ruin my press campaign. We talked further, and I discovered that he was under the impression that he'd been commissioned to shoot four Ziggy Stardust lookalikes for a fashion shoot. There was to be no interview. Clearly *The Face*'s system of communication was not as streamlined as its reputation as *the world's best-dressed magazine*. The doorbell rang. My heart sank.

The band arrived and I explained the situation. They all behaved impeccably—Brett shrugged, asked if there were any drugs around, and refused to wear any of the clothes on offer, as per usual; Mat thought the whole thing ridiculous with the air of someone who thought most things were ridiculous;* and Simon seemed terribly interested in the noises coming from the bedroom at the end of the corridor—apart from Bernard, who appeared to be in a heightened state of agitation. To his credit, he'd instinctively known something was up when he'd walked in

---

* Incidentally, Mat is responsible for one of my favourite ever ripostes:
  Brett: 'Mat, you smell like a horse's arse.'
  Mat: 'That's cos I'm wearing *Horse's Arse* by Lentheric.'

and noticed the clothes and then the state of the flat. And nothing was going to make him cooperate.

So stressful were the following few hours that I can't actually remember if anyone took any photographs; I was desperately trying to save the shoot, knowing that we'd never get offered six pages if we walked out of the building without making some kind of compromise. At one point, the two guys who'd been shagging each other in the bedroom walked out in their underpants, looked around in civil disinterest, lit each other's cigarettes, and walked back into the bedroom. Some drugs were ordered. Some drugs arrived. Some drugs were consumed. By this point, I was too distracted to care, since I'd spent the last hour trying on platforms and scarves and trying to convince the band that they'd look good in them. Bernard, in particular, was unimpressed.

Of course, you can see where Bernard's coming from: to whit, *I didn't get where I am today promoting my music by dressing up as a Ziggy Stardust lookalike*. OK, I get it. But there was something else about the incident that seemed to indicate that something else was going on: this was a press thing, and Bernard was a music thing. And never the twain shall meet.

The second incident occurred in August 1992, when Suede were due to be photographed for their first ever *NME* front cover. We'd already been at Steve Double's studio in the East End of London for several hours before Steve suggested that he take pictures of Brett and Bernard through a space in a large, dark grey piece of card that he'd fashioned into the shape of a cross. Bernard was having none of it, since the cross somehow represented the religion that he was in no hurry to mock: Catholicism. He refused to be photographed in this way, leaving all of us to wonder how Catholicism and his belief in it could survive this heretic development.

I have another theory: at the start of the photo session, Bernard had insisted that there were to be no individual shots of him or Brett, as it was important that they were always represented as a band. The cross, therefore, had thrown a spanner in the works; it meant that they would have to be photographed individually, as it was impossible to get both of them to stand behind the cross and look anything other than foolishly cramped. The cross also meant that the *NME* would now have a legitimate choice of putting one or the other of them on their front cover. And, to be brutal for a moment, one of those was not going to be Bernard.

Bernard left the session early, and Steve took a picture of Brett's floppy visage gazing out from behind the cross. The photograph surfaced on the cover of the following week's *NME*—just as Bernard had presumably predicted. Inadvertently, and despite Bernard's misgivings, a solo shot of Brett had now graced its first front cover, and he'd been thrust to the forefront of a press campaign that was only ever going to be driven by its most dominant common denominator. And Catholicism, surprisingly, had survived.

There's more to this than meets the eye. The music press and newspapers in general are not interested in writing about guitar lines and how they support and inspire the lyrical dexterity of a song. (There are magazines that do this, and they're called *Guitar* and *Guitarist*.) Instead, they want to write about the words of a song, the craft of a wordsmith, and the feelings those words generate. If you are a guitarist in a band and you want the music press to give you a 50–50 credit for writing a song—good luck, mate. The music press will always want the singer, not the song, and who knows where The Smiths would be now if Morrissey hadn't been lauded so far in excess of the Morrissey–Marr hybrid? And isn't this the reason why The Stone Roses split up after the first album? Or was that drugs? I can't remember.

And Bernard? He just wanted to be loved.

CHAPTER 7

THE CABINET

"When we arrive at the studio, Bowie is already there. He shakes hands with both of us before producing a contact sheet of a photo session he did with William Burroughs in 1973. He smells gorgeous and looks even better."

The March 20 1993 edition of the *NME* featured Brett Anderson and David Bowie on its cover. The concept had been the brainchild of *NME* editor Steve Sutherland—with a little help from Bowie himself—who had sent Bowie a cassette featuring the first two Suede singles, plus some bootleg material. 'Of all the tapes you've ever sent me, this is the only one I knew was instantly great,' Bowie told Sutherland, and then booked a studio in Primrose Hill so that he could play Brett his new album, *Black Tie, White Noise* (due to be released on April 5), and Brett could play him Suede's eponymous debut album (due for release a week prior).

When I speak to Brett about the forthcoming encounter he is nervous about meeting Bowie but also worried that Bowie's new record won't be any good, since his last two releases (as Tin Machine) weren't up to scratch. When we arrive at the studio, Bowie is already there. He shakes hands with both of us before producing a contact sheet of a photo session he did with William Burroughs in 1973. He smells gorgeous and looks even better.

'Tell you what,' he says to Brett. 'I'll be Bill and you be me.'

We are here to replicate a 1970s *NME* front cover shoot featuring Bowie and Burroughs, and Bowie is dressed as Burroughs in a grey suit, a thin-striped white shirt, and a fedora. It is cold, so Brett is wearing his customary black, furry coat. They do some photographs together in the yard outside the studio, sharing cigarettes and laughter. Then, back in the studio, Bowie plays several tracks from *Black Tie, White Noise*, and it's good. Brett tries not to look surprised, and they talk about the authenticity (or not) of some 70s music, the Smiths (Bowie has covered Morrissey's 'I Know It's Gonna Happen Some Day' on the album), sex, drugs, postmodernism, and Nazism. At one point, Brett says, 'When David started Tin Machine, it was the start of the cult of non-personality,' and when Bowie suggests magnanimously that 'your playing and your songwriting's so good that I know you're going to be working in music for quite some time', Brett appears unmoved. Interestingly, when Bowie maintains that Brett is in a position where he's 'not yet been pinned', Brett replies, 'Oh, there are people who want to pin us.'

Bowie seems surprised. 'Before the first album comes out! That's awful! That's a fast event horizon if ever there was one!'

You don't know the half of it, I'm thinking, but it is a highly amenable chat, and when it's over I rush my goodbyes and disappear back to the office so that I can boast about my day.

There's another reason why I am keen to leave: Steve Sutherland always makes me feel uncomfortable. Naturally, he has impeccable music taste, but I'd never had him down as a champion of fey indie causes, and once, when I was wearing some silk Japanese trousers from French Connection and walking ahead of him and up some stairs at an appropriately inappropriate indie club, I heard him say, 'What the fuck is Phill Savidge wearing?' It wasn't meant to be a compliment.

It can't have just been me that felt like this about Steve, as when he left *Melody Maker* to become *NME* editor in 1992, several people—including Andrew Collins, Stuart Maconie, Steve

Lamacq, and Mary Anne Hobbs—all resigned. This was political: Steve and several other members of the *Melody Maker* workforce had crossed an NUJ picket line earlier that year, and some *NME* staffers had not forgiven them. What's more, Steve had just penned a live review of Suede and Kingmaker—poor Kingmaker, always the bridesmaid—in the previous week's *Melody Maker*, under the banner headline 'PEARLS BEFORE SWINE', and that review's barbed witticisms had been seen as a direct attack on the *NME*: Suede were glamorous, sexy, exciting—*diamonds*—like *Melody Maker*, while Kingmaker were substandard *NME* fodder—*dog shit* was more than the implication.

When Steve arrived at his desk on his first day as editor of the *NME*, he found someone had blown up this review and pinned it on the door of his office. The irony is that this live review (with my best Suede hat on) is still pretty much my favourite Suede *critique* of all time—how could you not acknowledge the line 'What are Suede doing here, taunting the unconverted?' as one of the neatest ways to delineate the relationship between artist and potential fan?—and I'd had Steve's words pinned on the wall behind my desk ever since I'd grabbed hold of a copy of the paper on the previous Tuesday.

* * *

Five years later, in September 1998, I am looking after PR for Keith Allen, Damien Hirst, and Alex James as Fat Les. I am particularly close to Keith, but I like Damien a lot, too, and when he invites

SAVAGE & BEST

SUEDE - NEW PRICE LIST FOR 1999!

INTERVIEW SUBJECTS TO BE COVERED BY BRETT

MUSIC	FEE £5000
SEX	FEE £6000
GAY SEX	FEE £8000
BERNARD (NICE VERSION)	FEE £5000
BERNARD (NASTY VERSION)	FEE £10,000
DAMON	FEE £20,000
DAMON AND JUSTINE	FEE £35,000
JUSTINE	FEE £50,000

**BRETT AND JUSTINE TO TURN UP
AT PHOTO SESSION TOGETHER**   FEE £75,000

**BRETT AND JUSTINE
JOINT INTERVIEW**   FEE £35,000

**BRETT, JUSTINE AND SAM
CRACK SEX INTERVIEW**   FEE £100,000

SPECIAL OFFER - LIVE DRUG INTERVIEW   FEE £15,000
                     (PLUS PHOTOS)   FEE £30,000

*******LIVE CONCERTS*********LIVE CONCERTS************************

ATTENDANCE FEE	£100
REVIEWING FEE	£500
1ST 3 SONGS (NO PEN)	£200
LAST 2 SONGS (NO PAD)	£200

Phoners available upon request.

Discount for regular customers. Come in and see our new showroom in Camden and find out about some of our "real deals".

All cheques made payable to Savage and Best.

Savage & Best Ltd   79 Parkway   London   NW1 7PP   Tel 0171 482 7166   Fax 0171 482 7216   Accounts 0171 482 7105
Registered Office   Nettleton House   Calthorpe Road   Edgbaston   Birmingham   B15 1RL   Registered No 2708035   VAT No 564 4332 43

ADRIAN

ALISON

AMANDA

ANDREW

ANDY PERRY

Andy Ross the Boss.

annie

ANGI

ANKA

ANTHONY

ATTICUS

Ben Stud.

Bernard

BRIDGET

BRIX

Katie Pucknick
AKA: CAITLIN...

charlie.

CHLOE **Chris.** **CRAIG.** **CRiSPIN**

 ...  ...

DAMON. **DANNY** **DEAN.** **DEBBIE.**

DELE. DODGE & DARLING

THE DIVINE MS. M. Dom SLEEPY DONNA

EDDiE **EMMA** Everett **FLUFFY**

 ♥GRACIE

 GRAHAM & DAVE

 UP YOURS!
(Graham)

 Grandmistress

 HELEN

 IAN.

 MR. JARVIS COCKER

 JAIME

 JAMES.

 Jane.

 JASON

 Jefferson

 Jim.

 JONATHAN EDWARD BEST

 JOHN BOY HARRIS

 JOHN

JOHNNY.

JON SAVAGE

JUSTIN !

Justine

E. KATE

KLE the BEE

LIAM

LOZ.

Luke

MARIJNE

MARK .

McAlmont

Mr. Mark Sutherland

MARTIN A

MARTIN

MAT.

Matt.

M.ike

 Neil.

 PAT + JO, 'SKINNY'

 PAUL MATHUR

 el MOODY

 PEARL

 PETE TONG & PAUL McDONALD

 Philbert

 PHill...

PiERS

'Pink' FLOYD

 PoVVy.

RACHAEL

LEGS

 Richard

 RICHARD

 RUSKY

 RUSSELL

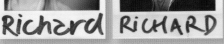

SARAH

SAUL.

Sian

Simon.

Simon.

Siobhan

sonya.

SOPH

SPLASH.

Stephen Duffy

STEVE

STEVOS

STUART.

Stuart.

in the pub all P.M.
SYLVIA

Ted.

TIM

TOMMY

Toni

William

PREVIOUS PAGES These polaroid pictures feature many of the people who passed through our offices during the 1990s. John and Polly took most of the pictures, and Polly has kept guard on them ever since. One notable absentee is Brett Anderson: this is explained by the fact that, as far as I recall, he only came to our offices on one occasion, for an *NME* photo session, and, as it was a Saturday and I was the only one there—and rarely take pictures—there is no polaroid of Brett in the collection. In truth, we used to admire Brett for hardly ever being seen in public—in shops or at pubs and nightclubs—and he only seemed to exist as a person you would see on TV or on stage. I think this made him more intriguing than any other artist of the era. **ABOVE** I took this picture of Brett and Neil Codling in March 1997 whilst in Hong Kong during Suede's *Coming Up* tour.

me to a launch at his Pharmacy restaurant in Notting Hill, I accept with the realisation that things are going to get messy. I am not the only invitee; Damien is the first of several European artists to create a piece of art for the *Absolut Originals Collection*, and this event is to help launch *Absolut Hirst*.

The Pharmacy has only been trading since January, but I am already a big fan. The last time I had dinner there with Keith, Bez from the Happy Mondays joined us and proceeded to take two ecstasy tablets during the entrée, and then act as if nothing untoward had happened throughout the rest of the meal. The place itself is achingly trendy: barstools are shaped like aspirins, packets of haemorrhoid cream and pillboxes sat in the window display, and when you go to the bathroom, the urinals are glass-backed, their insides stuffed with rubber gloves and syringes. More intriguing yet, when you order a cocktail—a Russian Quaalude or Anaesthetic Compound, perhaps—the drink is brought to your table by a glamorous woman—or man—dressed in a Prada-designed surgical gown. What is not to like?

At the *Absolut Hirst* launch, I sit on a small table with Polly, Rachel, and Damon Albarn. I don't know why I am sitting next to Damon, as we are supposed to be enemies of sorts—although we've never really had cross words, Damon is perennially jealous of the wall-to-wall press coverage Suede are awarded by the *NME* and *Melody Maker*, and he no doubt blames me for it. However, he and Polly are good friends, so he must have decided to overlook this fact for once.

The Pharmacy is buzzing, and there's an air of expectancy surrounding proceedings. I am just about to attempt small talk with Damon when I notice a commotion by the entrance: David Bowie has walked in, and there's a palpable intake of breath from all and sundry. Bowie walks straight over to our table and greets Damon warmly.

'Hello Damon,' he says. 'Really nice to meet you.' Then he turns to Polly, Rachel, and me, and says, 'And hello ladies!'

Great, I think. *I made a big impression there, then.*

Damon and Bowie chat for a few minutes before Bowie wanders off to greet someone else. Damon turns to Polly and whispers quietly, dramatically, in an absurdly high voice, '*David Bowie knows who I am!*' We all laugh.

Two hours elapse and I am getting on with Damon famously. I somehow find myself sitting on his lap. Damien has noticed our strange coupling and seems to find it funny, so he wanders over and attempts to French kiss me. It is playful, innocent stuff, but as I am fighting him off, I notice Bowie walking over. He is holding a video camera and, for one reason or another, filming the episode. I am embarrassed and attempt to climb off Damon's lap. After a while, Bowie gets bored and stops filming. I start to fantasise that I am about to become part of his video library.

I go on to work with Damien on something called *Art Tube*—a 2001 art exhibition where a working Piccadilly Line tube train exhibits specially commissioned panels by forty-two artists including Paul Simenon, Gavin Turk, Yoko Ono, John Cooper

Clarke, Jamie Reid, Vivienne Westwood, and Hirst himself—and *Glastonbury, The Play*, which was written by Zoe Lewis, directed by Keith Allen, and features Damien's extraordinary revolving stage designs. The latter becomes something of an obsession of mine, but it proves extraordinarily difficult to entice the usual theatregoing crowd into the marquees (with Portaloos) we have situated on the outskirts of cities such as Cardiff, Manchester, and Birmingham, and the non-theatregoing crowd—the *real* Glastonbury crowd, as it were—also seem peculiarly reticent to attend. Despite these projects, I can't say I know Damien that well, and when a guy called José Férez calls me up and says he has something that 'Damien will be interested in', I am as doubtful that I can help as I am that he is the genuine article.

José explains that he was a close friend and mentor of William Burroughs and that, when William died, he left many, many artefacts in José's possession. José invites me to his flat in Dalston, so that he can talk me through them.

One early evening the following week, I arrive at José's ground-floor flat to find him waiting on the doorstep, clutching a spliff. He offers me a smoke but I decline, so he invites me inside to peruse his Burroughs collection. As we talk, I realise that he is Mexican—not Spanish, as I had surmised during our phone conversation. He explains that he and Burroughs were close—very close—and I guess from José's age—he is around sixty—that José was Burroughs's younger lover, as well as his confidante. José is passionate about all aspects of the man, and his fingers play delicately on the myriad of canvases and manuscripts in his possession. He has literarily thousands of artefacts: original manuscripts in Burroughs's own handwriting; perhaps a hundred original paintings, each worth well over $10,000; shotguns and handguns; vials and syringes; window shutters that Burroughs has destroyed with gunfire; and yet more ephemera that any museum would have cut his right arm off for. He also has a Dreamachine, a stroboscopic flicker device (developed by Burroughs, fellow artist Bryon Gysin, and Burroughs's systems adviser, Ian Sommerville) that produces visual stimuli, and he explains that, when using it, one may enter a hypnagogic state, and that it is dangerous for people with photosensitive epilepsy or other nervous disorders. He also tells me that Kurt Cobain used to own one—there aren't many—and that one was found switched on in his house on the day he shot himself dead.

José shows me hundreds of photographs of him with Burroughs, together with the man himself and other artists and musicians such as Francis Bacon and Bryon Gysin, Kurt Cobain and Patti Smith. He even shows me pictures of Burroughs's funeral cortege stopping off at a McDonald's for refreshments—'William would have found it funny'—and of the funeral itself, where Patti is photographed placing a syringe and some heroin in the coffin. A shotgun is also placed with Burroughs in the casket.

I am astonished by what José has shown me, and I make several visits to his flat to document the collection. José and I strike up a friendship and spend many evenings together discussing Burroughs and his work. I am constantly making mental calculations to try to work out whether I can afford to buy a beautiful, hand-bound, boxed manuscript of *The Western Lands*, but it is $30,000 and out of my price range. I begin to understand that this is how José makes his money: when he is down on his luck, he sells some Burroughs's material and lives off the proceeds for the next few months. I agree to buy a signed, numbered, limited-edition copy of *The Seven Deadly Sins*— featuring seven multicolour shotgun woodblock screen-print images—for $1,000. In February 1991, Burroughs shot the front cover woodblock with a twelve-gauge shotgun.

During our conversations, José tells me that Burroughs was particularly close to Francis Bacon, whom he'd met in Tangier in the 1950s when he was writing *The Naked Lunch*. Subsequently, they hung out together at the Colony Room in the 60s, when Burroughs lived in London for a time. José knew that Damien was a huge admirer of Bacon's work—years later, Damien would see Bacon at the Colony Room but not speak to him, and would hail him as 'one of the greatest painters of all time, up there with Goya, Soutine, and Van Gogh'—and wondered if I knew what he thought of Burroughs, and whether indeed he was a fan. He explained that Burroughs had shot and painted nine full-size wooden doors in his lifetime, and that he wanted to sell one of them to Damien.

I ring Keith and ask him to find out whether Damien likes Burroughs, and he does. I tell José, and he asks me to arrange for

Damien to see the door. The process takes several weeks, since, by this time, Damien has moved to Devon and is spending most of his working week away from London.

Eventually, after much negotiation, Keith, Damien, and I meet on a rain-sodden Thursday evening at the Groucho before climbing into a black cab and heading to José's apartment. By this time, José has also moved, so we head for his new apartment in South Lambeth. Despite the use of a taxi, we arrive comically soaked, and there is much laughter when we emerge into the light of José's living room looking like homeless urchins. José serves drinks then shows us down a corridor so that we can see the Burroughs door.

I notice a framed photograph of Ryan Giggs on the wall of the corridor; it depicts his naked, hairy chest, and he's waving his shirt around his head after his decisive winning goal in the Manchester United–Arsenal semi-final at Villa Park in 1991.

'I didn't think you liked football?' I say to José.

'I don't,' he says, and gives me a coy smile. 'But you know …'

By now, Keith and Damien have spotted the door, which is standing up against the frame of a doorway, almost as if it has been cut out of the doorway itself. It is exactly as I imagined it to be: great swirls of paint, seemingly random in composition, occupy most of the surface, and there are countless scraggy holes—presumably the result of Burroughs's shotgun ire—dotted all over its surface. Damien disappears behind the door, and after a few moments I notice some sort of pink object poking through one of the biggest holes in the door. It is Damien's cock. José starts to laugh uncontrollably and pulls out a camera to start taking pictures. Keith makes a lunge for Damien's appendage, but he pulls it away from the hole just in time.

Damien obviously likes the door, because a few months later José calls me to say that he has bought a shutter and the door for a substantial sum of money. José thanks me profusely and asks me to come over to his apartment, where he has a present for me. The next day, I head over to South Lambeth, fantasising that José is going to give me the boxed manuscript of *The Western Lands*. Instead, when I arrive, he unveils a screen print created by Ralph Steadman and shot up (by a variety of ammunition) by both him and Burroughs at the latter's home in Lawrence, Kansas. The print is numbered, limited, and titled *Something New Has Been Added*. It has been signed ostentatiously by both Burroughs and Steadman, and it features etchings of Burroughs's face either side of a target painted by Steadman.

Although I was gunning—ha!—for some of Burroughs's rarest written works, I am not altogether disappointed by my 'gift', as I have come to look fondly on his etchings, sketches, and amateur doodles, and I now see them as things of beauty. José packs my screen-print away carefully, and I take it home so it can take pride of place on my walls.

I don't hear from José again for several weeks, but when I do he tells me that Damien has been in touch and offered to build him a cabinet so that José can house his favourite pieces of Burroughs memorabilia. Damien makes several visits to José's apartment—he's now moved back to Dalston—and it is here that he comes across a piece of paper with the words *I'll be right back* written on it. These were the last words spoken by Burroughs inside the ambulance as he was taken to hospital; José had written them down and kept them—along with the other papers from the time of his death—inside a box, together with earth from his grave. Damien decides that this will be the title of his artwork.

Damien chooses which pieces of Burroughs ephemera should be placed in the cabinet. These include targets and bullet shells; Burroughs's last dose of methadone in its original bottle; small, signed literary editions; two containers featuring 916 of José's photos of Burroughs and his world during the last ten years of his life (including some from his wake and funeral); handwritten cards; a tape of Burroughs reading his essay 'The Four Horseman Of The Apocalypse'; a railways spike that he saw in a dream (and that latterly he and José had found by the tracks); and some 'secret agent' eyeglasses that Burroughs had given to José.

José is extremely excited by Damien's generosity and attention to detail, and we discuss the value of the cabinet on the understanding that it will never be sold. I tell José that Damien donates many pieces of art to his friends but doesn't look kindly on those who make a profit from selling them on. José reminds me that Damien's glass drug cabinet, *God, 1989*, had shelves lined with medicine bottles like the ones in Pharmacy and sold via Christies, whilst I point out that Damien managed to sell the entire contents of Pharmacy in 2004 for $11 million after its closure. When I tell him that one collector paid £4,000 for a pair of Martini glasses and another paid £55,000 for a neon sign with the word *prescriptions* on it, José looks at me like his life is about to take a turn for the better.

A few years later, in April 2008, José and I travel to Dublin to visit the Irish Museum of Modern Art, which is holding an exhibition focusing on the cut-outs and cut-ups of Hans Christian Andersen and Burroughs. They are billed as *incredibly productive and revolutionary writers who made beautiful and challenging artworks and were visual thinkers whose writings and drawings were intimately connected*, but I fail to see the connection; I am only here because I have heard the *freestanding, kinetic Dreamachine* will be in attendance, and it is a chance to see the contraption in a working environment. When I track it down in one of the furthest reaches of the museum, it is surrounded by interested parties standing around with their eyes closed. It's a pretty unimpressive piece of technology—like a homemade lampshade based on something from a 1970s Habitat store catalogue—even in this environment, but I attempt to become bedazzled nonetheless. This involves me standing in front of the Dreamachine with my eyes closed, but I see neither bright patterns of colour nor lights shimmering behind my eyelids. Nor do I feel nauseous, just a little idiotic and extremely self-conscious. I open my eyes and notice José smiling at me.

Later that year, I have several meetings with the Royal Academy, which is due to hold a *Burroughs Live* Exhibition in January of the following year. The exhibition is curated by José, marks fifty years since the publication of Naked Lunch, and 'brings together self portraits, films, and works inspired by Burroughs from artists like Damien Hirst, Annie Leibovitz, and David Hockney'. It will also be the first time *I'll Be Right Back* makes a public appearance.

I am extremely excited by the exhibition and the prospect of the cabinet being shown in public. I devise a plan to persuade a host of musicians (who have a strong Burroughs connection) to perform at the Royal Academy during the opening week of the exhibition. I tell José, and he thinks it's a great idea. I check the feasibility of live performances at the Academy with the Academy itself, but they maintain it is impossible to use any of their spaces for this purpose. I source a nearby chapel, and they seem keen to help out. I draft and send a letter to the musicians on my hit list: Patti Smith, Tom Waits, R.E.M., Thurston Moore, The Klaxons, Nick Cave, David Bowie, Debbie Harry, The Horrors, Genesis P. Orridge, Lou Reed, Laurie Anderson—the list is seemingly endless. Some of these artists show some interest, but I hear from a source close to Bowie that he won't be travelling to London in the foreseeable future, and he certainly won't be performing live ever again. For some reason, this news makes me lose heart in the venture.

I attend the launch party for *Burroughs Live*—an event that appears, to me at least, to be conspicuously lacking a live performance element. At one point, I stand as close to the cabinet as tactful discretion allows and watch people's reactions

as they walk up to it and peer at the description beneath. I notice
Malcolm McLaren do just this, turn to his companion, and
mutter something indecipherable. José notices this too and begins
a conversation with Malcolm. He looks relaxed and happier than
I have ever seen him.

Later that year, José and I travel to Paris, as he wants to show
me some works by the Japanese artist Kenji Yoshida. Yoshida died
in February; José was extremely close to him, and is still deeply
saddened by his death. I like his paintings—giant oil on canvas
contraptions incorporating abstract shapes on a grand scale—
but when José tells me that Yoshida was conscripted in 1943,
earmarked to be a kamikaze pilot, but never got round to it due to
Japan being defeated, I seem to find this funny: a failed kamikaze
pilot! Later, José explains that Yoshida had always planned to crash
his plane into the sea so that he didn't kill anyone.

I return to London alone, as José wants to remain in Paris to
pack and archive the contents of Yoshida's studio. When we say
goodbye, he looks slightly bewildered, lost amongst the debris
of his friend's belongings. Just over a year later, after several
unreturned emails and phone calls, I decide to google his name.
And there it is: José Ferez Kuri, curator and author: born Mexico
City, March 19 1951; died Paris, March 25 2010. He'd only just
turned fifty-nine.

I receive this news almost six months after José's death, so I am
unsure how to react. Naturally, I am upset, and a wave of sadness
forces me to stare off into space for several minutes, but I can't

help thinking that I am less sad than I should be. Is this because he has been dead for such a long time without my knowledge? Is it possible that I think I can achieve nothing for either of us by grieving so long after the event? And how close were he and I anyway, since I never met any other members of his family and was never contacted about his death? And what does this say about me?

I learn that José had a series of heart attacks before he died, and that a photograph of José and Burroughs at the latter's eightieth birthday party, together with a Yoshida painting, was placed in the coffin at his funeral at Père Lachaise cemetery. I also learn that José was one of ten children from a Lebanese/Mexican family, and that he was 'at the centre of a vast group of friends'. I realise that I knew nothing about his family and had never met anyone else from this vast group of friends. It is almost as if José and I had conducted a series of secret assignations together.

In 2014, the cabinet is put up for sale by the auction house Phillips. The catalogue states, 'Damien Hirst. *I'll Be Right Back*: Portrait of William Burroughs. MDF cabinet with assorted found objects, glass shelves, and doors with lock. Signed, titled, dedicated, and dated *Hirst, I'll be right back, portrait of William Burroughs, for José, Damien Hirst, 3rd May 2004, for José!* on the reverse.' It is estimated at $150,000–200,000, and sells for $182,500.

CHAPTER 8

THE DRUGS DO NOT WORK

"For the record, I have never been interested in managing an artist—I'm far too busy imagining I am an artist myself and worrying about my hair—and the constant intimacy related to the manager—artist relationship fills me with dread."

Maybe only a fantasist would suggest that I was in any way involved in (The) Verve's management, since it was all John's work at the outset—although Sue Whitehouse worked alongside John on the management side of the company. For the record, I have never been interested in managing an artist—I'm far too busy imagining I am an artist myself and worrying about my hair—and the constant intimacy related to the manager–artist relationship fills me with dread. I remember being in Paris with Suede, and their loveable manager, Charlie Charlton, cancelling a plane on the hour, every hour, for an entire day due to the very real non-arrival of Brett in the land of wakefulness. I had spent much of the previous evening—and, indeed, the following morning—at an outrageously decadent party with Brett and the rest of the band, and I couldn't envisage being the person who had to organise getting his life back on track; I think I always wanted to be the one whose life needed to be organised by someone else.

I liked Verve and had done so since seeing them at a small club called the Dome in Tufnell Park in the early 1990s. The band performed as if there were hundreds, or perhaps thousands, present. There weren't. Indeed, there must have been no more than twenty people scattered around the rather neglected and, I thought at the time, unloved venue. Richard Ashcroft—Verve's frontman—in particular was an incredibly confident stage presence, crouching down as if possessed of some demonic spirit he wanted to exorcise. From a press point of view, I knew they'd do well enough, although John fell in love with them to such an extent that you could sense he wanted to become as intimately involved as possible. For my part, I could tell the band liked John more than me, but I felt no antipathy; better to remain at arm's length, I thought, than swim with the sharks. Or angry, northern fish, at least.

In 1992, we managed to secure some great press coverage for the band's first few EPs—*All In The Mind*, *She's A Superstar*, and *Gravity Grave*—but the press lumped the band in with every other movement—shoegazing, The Scene That Celebrates Itself, Camden—that we were associated with. The last of these was particularly galling, since the band hailed from Wigan, and when Britpop started to consume all those around it, I could tell Verve were beginning to grow apart from the music business. Having said that, Verve gigs were often interminable affairs involving guitar solos that didn't know where they were going and songs that appeared to have no meaning. This may have had something to do with the fact that the band had spent so long listening to (and hanging round with) Spiritualized that they believed the best way to entertain an audience was to play for so long that they'd forget why they'd come to the gig in the first place. As much as I liked the band, they didn't really move me to a place where I wanted to be.

In June 1993, our beloved Verve were forced to change their name to The Verve. The reason? Veteran US jazz label Verve Records was concerned that people would confuse Verve with

Verve Records and come to the wrong purchasing decisions. The case was settled out of court, but I could only speculate as to the legal exchange that would have ensued if it hadn't been.

'Did you or did you not attempt to buy a jazz recording on the day in question?'

'I did.'

'And can you describe to this court the situation that ensued?'

'I can and will attempt to do so now. On the day in question I had lunched most satisfactorily and wondered whether I should taxi home immediately or wander amongst some of my more excellent Soho bedfellows with a view to pursuing further merriment. All right, I admit to this court that I was smitten— smitten with a love of jazz, not just jazz as my contemporaries might view it—oh, how I hate modern jazz!—but jazz as my father loved. Trad jazz. Big-band jazz. Jazz as it was envisaged in the 1930s and 1940s. And as I was staggering home I saw Ray's Jazz Shop on the corner of Shaftsbury Avenue, and I knew I had to go in.'

'And what happened then?'

'Well, I asked for the latest Verve record, and to my horror and surprise the man reached under the counter and pulled out a twelve-inch single by a band called Verve. Perhaps he'd also been duped—I don't know—but I didn't say anything, as I presumed it must be some contemporaneous jazz outfit I should already be aware of. Imagine my surprise, however, when I arrived home and attempted to play the record: it was undeniably not a jazz recording, instead the meaningless meanderings of a bunch of musicians attempting to achieve soporific flight—possibly in an attempt to emulate their heroes, a band called Spiritualized, who I admit I have never heard of but believe to be an outfit they have toured with on several occasions. Indeed, isn't it true to say that Verve—oh how strange and un-jazz-like that name seems now!—and Spiritualized share the same PR company?'

'And would you say you were coerced into buying this record and indeed misled by the band's name?'

'I would, and I'd go further: unless this band changes their name, thousands of jazz fans will innocently walk into record shops all over the country and ask for the latest Verve record. On these occasions they will receive no jazz whatsoever whilst this so-called band Verve will get richer and richer and lonelier and lonelier and be forced to pursue their career even more vigorously. The result will be that we shall be forced to countenance their fatuous nonsense for even longer.'

'And how will this situation affect the jazz community as a whole?'

'Well, the consequences will be catastrophic: the jazz musicians we know and love will become poorer and poorer and lonelier and lonelier until they are forced to play other types of music other than jazz to make ends meet.'

'So you could say that unless this band defers from masquerading as a jazz label by using the name Verve, it will mean the very death of jazz itself?'

'Those are your words not mine, my learned friend, but, yes, it would mean the very death of jazz itself.'

In the end, I think that sums up Verve—or The Verve (and thank you for that, our legal brethren)—perfectly, don't you? Far from being Britpop-denier pioneers or prog-pop playmakers, they were the very death of jazz itself.

I thought Richard Ashcroft a sweetheart, mind you, although he did seem bemused by all the activities going on in our office—as I was, most of the time—and often appeared several days later than he was supposed to and not wearing any shoes. I don't think any of this was contrived. I think that's just the way he was.

One day in 1996, he turned up in the office after attending one (or both) of the Balloch Country Park shows that Oasis headlined at Loch Lomond on August 3 and 4 of that year. He seemed agitated and, when pressed, revealed that the festival had changed his perspective on the music business. Liam and Noel were now perhaps role models as well as friends, he implied, and their manager, Marcus Russell, had pulled off a coup when he'd had cash machines flown into the arena so that Oasis fans could access their savings and spend it on Oasis merchandise. In these enlightened times, this is normal procedure, but Richard was particularly impressed by the practise and suggested that any manager worth his salt should be able to do the same for him. Would Savage & Best be able to assure him that we'd be able to provide the same kind of services once Verve had made the leap from venue to festival to stadium?

Naturally, Richard's inquisition was part of a wider malaise: he'd had his head turned by seeing his contemporaries become hugely successful and wanted to make sure he had the best team in place so that he could join them as soon as possible. I knew we were the best music PR company in Britain, but I could understand his reticence otherwise: we had no track record of managing anyone, just making people famous. The writing was on the wall.

* * *

The following year, Richard played a cassette of 'Bitter Sweet Symphony' in the office, and I was absolutely smitten. It felt like a game-changer, and yet something still felt wrong: the demo was messy and almost twenty minutes in length, and I couldn't be sure that there weren't several versions of it that we were meant to separate into good and bad. Of course, shortly after this, I realised that I had somehow heard it all before, and when the band were sued for using an Andrew Loog Oldham sample, I knew my first instinct had been correct.

On June 16 1997, The Verve released 'Bitter Sweet Symphony' and the song went 'straight' to no.2 in the charts.* It subsequently

---

* Incidentally, one of my big bugbears is that I can't stand it when record companies, press officers, and journalists, in particular, say that a song went 'straight in' to the charts at no.1, since by the time the 1990s kicked in—due to sophisticated marketing techniques and front-loaded press, TV, radio, and advertising strategies well in advance of a single's release—a record's highest position was always going to be in its first week of release, so 'straight in' becomes something of a redundant expression.

hung around the upper regions of the charts for a further three months—a huge amount of time for anything released in an era of instant love and instant dismissal—and it was obvious that the song had become a word of mouth phenomenon. By this time, of course, the band had appointed Jazz Summers—a man you could rely on to commandeer cash machines at a moment's notice—as manager, but the band were also embroiled in a bitter dispute with the pre-1970s Rolling Stones' management over the origins of the song. The Stones' management won: the string passage that defined 'Bitter Sweet Symphony' was deemed to have had its origins in a symphonic Loog Oldham version of the Stones' 'The Last Time', and Jagger and Richards would subsequently claim 100 percent of the publishing. The Verve had to relinquish all royalties, and the credits for the song were changed to Jagger/ Richards/Ashcroft.

I suddenly felt glad to be out of the picture, except I could never fully escape the grasp of the band, because 'Bitter Sweet Symphony' was everywhere—even if it had been kept off the top slot by 'I'll Be Missing You', Puff Daddy and Faith Evans's tribute to The Notorious B.I.G. Every store I went into at the time seemed to be playing the song, and the fact that it got marooned at no.2 meant that there was a groundswell of support for the record that felt unprecedented. 'Shit, they have the sympathy vote as well as the symphony vote,' I once joshed, but it felt like a bittersweet irony for all concerned, since the band weren't earning any money from the song, and Savage &

Best were about to play no part in their instant notoriety and perceived success.

I was also aggrieved as my Second Proper Girlfriend had just left me after five years. This hit me particularly hard, as I hadn't seen it coming. The split, though amicable, had been instigated by her, due to the fact that she had become bored of everyone presuming we were girlfriends. When she suggested that we split up, I had nodded as if in agreement on what takeaway to order that evening, but we decided to carry on living together until we'd both made other arrangements.

This was a big mistake. I carried on as if nothing had really changed, and after a couple of weeks she accused me of behaving as if nothing had really changed. At this point, I made a fulsome effort to alter my appearance and went to a painfully hip Shoreditch salon to have my hair cut off. I asked them to make me look like an 'aristocratic supermodel'—and handed over a picture of Stella Tennant—but when I took a cab back to our apartment, the driver asked me if I was going to meet my boyfriend.

One night, whilst my (now ex) Second Proper Girlfriend was on a press trip in the USA, I returned home and put the key in the front door of our empty apartment. We lived on the first floor of a house in Muswell Hill, and I was only vaguely aware of the middle-aged Asian woman who lived downstairs, having noticed the significant number of young men who had passed through her apartment over the last two years.

Tonight, she appeared to be having a very good time. As I opened the door and climbed the stairs, I could hear raised voices and glasses clinking over recorded music. Then there was silence, and the sound of someone fiddling with an acoustic guitar. A man started to sing, and I stopped momentarily, as his amateur strumming suddenly seemed familiar. It couldn't be, could it? But no, there it was again, the distinctive sound of someone singing The Verve's next single, 'The Drugs Don't Work'. This seemed terribly unlikely, as the song wasn't due to be released for at least six weeks, and the woman downstairs couldn't possibly have bumped into someone who knew the song so intimately. A thought struck me: could Richard Ashcroft himself be downstairs, serenading my neighbour?*

Naturally, this was not the case, but the man continued to play 'The Drugs Don't Work' on his guitar for several hours,

* When I moved to a converted church in Crouch End, Fran Healy from Travis moved in next door, and I used to see him and his wife, Nora, when I came back from work most days. It felt appropriate that two stalwarts of the Britpop era should live next door to each other. One Friday night, however, I got even more wasted than usual and spent the early part of the morning struggling to get to sleep. It must have been around 10am when I heard some god-awful band murdering Travis's 'Why Does It Always Rain On Me?' in the local park of which the church formed part.

Christ, I thought. *That is beyond embarrassing. Fran's not ten meters from this house and he has to put up with some dreadful covers band ruining his songs.* Several more abysmal versions of Travis material followed before I drifted off to sleep. I resolved to have words with the local council to ensure that further embarrassment was avoided when Prince moved into the flat above.

Naturally, when I picked up a copy of *The Sun* on Monday morning, I noticed the headline immediately: 'Kids' joy as rock stars Travis play local park'.

occasionally pausing so that the pair of them could laugh and sing together. At one point they appeared to make all the appropriate noises suggesting they were having sex whilst listening to a recording of the song, but I couldn't work out how they got hold of a cassette or CD as no music had ever left our office. The only explanation was that The Verve were now so enormous that everyone in the world knew all the words to their songs weeks in advance of their release.

And we'd been fired.

On September 1 1997, The Verve released 'The Drugs Don't Work'. It went to no.1. Princess Diana had died the day before the song's release and she was buried the following Saturday. The country was in a peculiar state of dysphoria, as indeed was I, as I'd liked her ever since she replied to a letter a friend of mine had sent to her when we were at school. My Second Proper Girlfriend and I had agreed on several occasions that she was a much maligned individual—I still remember that, on the Sunday before her death, a British newspaper had remarked on her recent acquisition of cellulite, as if the existence of such a thing should negate her worth—but I now sensed that she was leaving both me and her country in our hour of need.

On October 6, The Verve released their third album, *Urban Hymns*, the first album without Savage & Best as their management team. I have to assure you that even though I was never part of their management team, I felt the loss nonetheless. My Second Proper Girlfriend ran off—I always find they run off, rather than saunter—to America and married someone else whilst we were still living together. I can't really blame her. *Urban Hymns* reached no.1 and stayed on the album chart for the next three years. The band has split up and reformed several times since. Oh, and for the record, Verve Records, despite the confusion, still survives.

CHAPTER 9

RAZZAMATAZZ

"I used to own an antique Porsche, and I can imagine that on several occasions it could have been described as *gleaming*."

'On time to the minute, a gleaming antique Porsche draws up to the kerb and a very glamorous pop person in heavy slap and earrings steps out. It is the PR. Jarvis, in thick specs and belted granny cardie, unravels from the passenger seat.'
—Lynn Barber, *The Observer*, April 5 1998

I used to own an antique Porsche, and I can imagine that on several occasions it could have been described as *gleaming*. I can particularly envisage the *gleaming* description being applied appropriately whenever I had to deliver one of the artists I represented to a journalist who was about to interview him or her. These were the occasions that prompted me to have the car cleaned inside and out. I wanted both Jarvis and Lynn Barber— the journalist who was due to interview the Pulp frontman—to be comfortable. It was a mark of genuine respect to her and to him.

Having said all that, I remember reading these three sentences when they were first published in *The Observer*'s *Life* magazine and wondering what Lynn was trying to say. On the one hand, she was naturally pointing out that Jarvis Cocker was untouched by fame—unlike his PR, presumably—and turned up for interviews in 'a belted cardie', as if he didn't care what journalists or the general public thought of him. And then there was the description of Jarvis unravelling himself from the passenger seat, as if he'd been ravelled in the first place. *So, how did he get ravelled?* was the implication. Did he do this to himself, due to some unspecified ineptitude? Barber is a quite brilliant journalist, and nothing escapes her gaze, so the *unravelling* comment was surely part of her scheme to expose Jarvis's ungainliness and set the scene for another celebrated Barber encounter with another celebrated celebrity.

And then of course, there's the car itself—*a gleaming antique Porsche*—which Jarvis is not driving. This is confusing: is he too famous to drive, or can he not drive at all? Perhaps he is too poor to drive a car like this but rich enough to employ a driver? The person driving is *a very glamorous pop person in heavy slap and earrings*, but there is no reference to the gender of the driver. They are simply a *person*. Why is this? At the time, I wondered whether Barber was confused as to my real gender, but this did not make any sense: we'd had several conversations on the phone where she no doubt assumed me to be male, and when I had turned up with Jarvis and stepped out of my car—note the clever, almost androgynous, slightly feminine reference to *stepping* out rather than *climbing*, *leaping*, or *jumping* out—she might have thought Jarvis had arrived with a girl friend. But my manner was familiar enough to be intimately related to the *person* she had spoken to on previous occasions, so there was little likelihood she could have been confused.

But then again, *IT IS THE PR!?* How awkward must it have been to refer to me using third-person, gender-neutral terminology? I am wondering, if I had been identifiably either female or male in Lynn's eyes, whether she would ever have referred to me in this way. But what were the alternatives? *She is the PR* would have made the *heavy slap and earrings* reference appear bitchy and unnecessary. And *he is the PR* would have spoiled whatever illusion Lynn was trying to create, forcing her readers to focus on the anomaly—a man wearing makeup and earrings—delivering Jarvis to her cosy abode. So, in hindsight, *it is the PR* seems to be just about perfect.

Of course, hindsight is a wonderful thing, and I was amused to hear later that Barber rang fellow *Observer* journalist Miranda Sawyer to ask what my 'story' was as soon as she had finished the interview. When Miranda presumably told her that I was just androgynous and didn't mind the confusion my appearance generated, she must have decided to describe me in the terms detailed above. Perhaps she could have made no reference to me whatsoever, but the contrast between my pompous asexuality and Jarvis's newfound cool must have proved too difficult to resist. *It,* after all, is the journalist's prerogative.

Incidentally, I should probably point out that my ownership of the Porsche—actually a 1977 Porsche 911 Targa version with an orange art-deco interior—had proved to be a confusing entity for all concerned: not only had a chap in a Mercedes exclaimed *rich bitch* with unusual abandon when I'd sidled up next to him at a set of traffic lights, but my presence at a V Festival—which Savage & Best had been charged to represent—had enabled the following scenario to take place.

'Oh, you're the lady that Gavin sold his Porsche to!' suggested the poshest woman I'd ever met (presumably Gavin's wife or girlfriend), when I'd encountered her along the side of a backstage trailer at the festival. 'It's so lovely to meet you,' she continued. 'Gavin told me all about you!'

Evidently not! I thought.

When I explained that I had lost my keys between the car park and the backstage area, she gallantly leapt to my defence, disappeared into a cabin, and grabbed the microphone connected to the backstage Tannoy system. The next thing I knew, she was shouting into the microphone as if she was borne to the airwaves of Posh FM.

'Ladies and gentleman,' she offered to the assembled hordes. 'A lady back here has misplaced the keys to her Porsche, so if any of you come across them, please bring them into the production office.' I cringed with embarrassment, and yet now, when I think about such things, I wonder what I was embarrassed about.

Naturally, Lynn Barber knew nothing about this when we agreed that Jarvis should be interviewed at her house. Even here, however, I have to claim some self-interest. Or was it thinly disguised PR interest in making Jarvis appear in the best light possible?

'Where shall we do the interview?' Lynn had asked me, when we'd finally established (via her editor) that a Lynn Barber–Jarvis Cocker encounter was actually going to take place.

'Well, we could do it in a café, or in Jarvis's house,' I suggested. 'But why don't we do it at your house?'

I could tell this was a novel approach by the silence on the other end of the line.

'Oka—hay,' she said. 'That would be really nice.'

I had been a fan of Lynn Barber's journalism for quite some time, marvelling at the unique observatory nature of her writing. Barber was an expert at noticing the eccentricities and idiosyncrasies of everyone she interviewed, and I knew there was only one winner when it came to one of her profiles—and that was Lynn Barber herself. I wondered, therefore, whether the reason for this inevitable outcome was that Lynn always felt comfortable in surroundings that were unfamiliar to herself and to her victims. Here, in the café or restaurant, or perhaps even in the gardens of a stately home or during a walk along a busy canal towpath, Barber could observe the subjects of her interviews in a truly neutral environment, all the better to capture the essence of her prey. The interviewee is only too aware that he or she is being watched, and is liable to behave accordingly; perhaps he or she might even act with such peculiar, self-conscious abandon that Barber would feel compelled to comment on the unusual nature of their activities. This potential scenario, I calculated wisely, on being a student of her interviews, was a situation to be avoided.

But imagine if the interview had taken place at Jarvis's house. Lynn would have noted the way Jarvis lived, and perhaps fundamentally how he had ended up at this stage of his life. She would have examined his bookshelves and his kitchen, his living room, and his bathroom—and, more pertinently, how he interacted within his domestic environment. This would surely have revealed too much to the general public. Jarvis would be only too aware that he was being interviewed in his own house and act in an unusually self-conscious manner, rather like the subject of an experiment being affected by the experiment itself; perhaps he might have been more affectionate to his cat than was necessary, or insisted—with such unnatural kindness!—that Lynn make herself more comfortable. This would make her feel doted upon, and force her to comment on Jarvis's lack of natural social or intuitive skills. And what of the room he'd picked for the interview itself? The kitchen? Too untidy! The living room? Too much information! The bedroom? Far too intimate!

Interestingly enough, Barber, in her excellent article, comments on the unusual nature of the interview scenario. 'And now he is coming to breakfast,' she writes. 'This is a sort of fugue experience because I spent an embarrassingly large part of my teens and twenties fantasising that a pop star was coming to breakfast.' And then, perhaps disingenuously, she adds, 'Quite why Jarvis is coming to breakfast remains a mystery—his PR minders wanted us to meet in a caff but I refused (risk of being mobbed by fans)—so Monday morning finds me whirling round the house in a complete tizz, hiding the potpourri (he told *The Face* that potpourri, along with Belgian chocolates, counted as his "worst fear") and double-checking that I haven't suddenly acquired a copy of *A Year In Provence*.'

Apart from the gross misrepresentation (and herein lies the writer's immunity) that Jarvis's *PR minders*—I'd dearly love to meet this bunch of miscreant hoodlums, as perhaps they are all wearing heavy slap and earrings—had suggested a caff—the vernacular is presumably intended to undermine the interrogation process, and to belittle the venue as a meeting place—I think this is a fascinating section of the interview. However, 'Quite why Jarvis is coming to breakfast remains a mystery?' is one of the most outrageous sentences published in the English language. I think we all know why Jarvis is coming to breakfast! To hoist you with your own petard, Ms Barber! And though Lynn is *whirling round the house in a complete tizz*, I am entitled to have very little sympathy.

At the next juncture, Lynn says, 'I find it quite confusing trying to combine the roles of interviewer and hostess, but he makes it easy—he is so likeable. All he wants for breakfast is old-fashioned tea and toast. He comes into the kitchen and rabbits on while I make it.' Whilst reading (and re-reading) Lynn's article, I was very glad to hear that Lynn had found the situation confusing, since this was my intention all along. And I think we'd all agree that combining the roles of interviewer and hostess must be a very confusing scenario indeed; on the one hand, Lynn has to concentrate on engaging with Jarvis and making sure she asks him some pertinent questions, and on the other hand, she has to worry about the state of her house and what Jarvis might think about it. It's a wonder she could put pen to paper and accurately describe anything that occurred during the entire episode.

And, of course, whilst this is all occurring, there's an unseen, unspoken drama going on elsewhere—namely, where I was when

Lynn was interviewing Jarvis in her kitchen? For I, dear reader, was defiantly sitting bolt upright on Lynn's bed in her bedroom upstairs. Quite how this had happened is difficult to fathom, but I think Lynn was so flustered by the presence of Jarvis in her house that she couldn't think of anywhere else to put me, other than her bedroom. She offered me a vodka and tonic, which I accepted, even though it was eleven o'clock in the morning. And whilst nothing sinister was going on—I actually read a copy of that day's newspaper and sipped my vodka and tonic—it is easy to see why she admits in the piece that whilst 'trying to make breakfast and do five things at once' she was 'not really paying attention'. Indeed, it is difficult to see how she could think of anything else other than the presence of Jarvis's PR (of indeterminate gender) sitting on her bed in her bedroom.

Naturally, I survived Lynn's interrogation, but I am not sure that my relationship with Jarvis did. By which I mean to say that although he may have come over as a jolly loveable chap in the interview, I don't think he quite approved of me being called *glamorous* in the first place. This is understandable—a PR should never get in the way of the story—but perhaps it was the fact that I picked him up in a Porsche that upset him even more. Our acquaintance would be distinctly frostier from that point on.

Well, not quite.

On June 28 1998, Pulp were due to play Glastonbury Festival, and I was along for the ride. The band hadn't played the festival since 1995, when they'd stood in for The Stone Roses at the last minute and astonished most of the media by actually carrying it off. I wasn't sure they could pull it off either—I mean, everyone in the office loved them, but we couldn't guarantee we weren't living in a bubble—and I was worried that the festival was going to be full of pissed-up Mancs expecting The Stone Roses and shouting, 'Fuck off, you poof.' In fact, I couldn't guarantee they wouldn't be shouting this at me. My real fear, however, was that they might get bottled off. But from the minute they opened up with 'Do You Remember The First Time?' and then 'Razzamatazz', I knew they were going to be all right.

Actually, Pulp were more than all right that weekend—they were so good it felt like they'd been beamed down from another planet, which is more than can be said for their erstwhile PR associate, who was in the usual state of festival disrepair, the result of consuming too many drugs and combining this with no sleep and only eating one strawberry, which I'd been force-fed by Crispin from The Longpigs, all weekend.* *Twas ever thus*, I hear you cry, but really my relationship with Glastonbury hadn't been on firm ground since my first visit with Suede. I remember standing next to the *NME*'s John Mulvey—who had put Brett and Bernard on

---

* The first time I met Longpigs main-man Crispin Hunt—who had just signed with Savage & Best—he spoke to me for several minutes after confusing me with a woman he knew back in Sheffield. He was mortified when his girlfriend, Rachael, told him I was the person he'd wanted to do his PR since the band's inception; paradoxically, of course, Crispin presumed his career to be over due to this misunderstanding, not realising I was perfectly happy with the delusion and now planned to make his career my priority.

the cover the week before—and, as they were playing 'Still Life', saying to him, 'Aren't they astonishing? Cover next week?' and John saying, 'Yeah, all right then.' There was surely jesting involved on John's part, but in that moment I inhabited an endless loop where Suede were on the *NME* cover every week, each time performing live and headlining the most perfect festival that heaven could allow. Despite the illusion, I was only too aware that the reality of Glastonbury meant that I had spent much of an earlier visit in the Samaritans Tent, a consequence of being abandoned by a girl I was in love with but had failed to put up a tent for correctly.

By the time June 28 1998 arrived, I'd just had about enough of Glastonbury, but I decided that I could cushion the emotional blow of being surrounded by the loneliness generated by two hundred thousand festivalgoers—oh yes, I can be poetic if I want to be— by planning three forms of accommodation for the weekend. I arrived with a close female friend—who I am sure I regarded as a girlfriend at the time—in a Winnebago, and then put up a tent— don't panic, I'd practised putting up several tents in my bedroom after the last incident—before confirming my reservation at Soho House's country hotel offshoot, Babington House.

Of course, on the evening of Pulp's performance, there were very few organisational niceties to be negotiated; the band may have performed more sublimely than in 1995, but I still gave my tent to a very grateful, very out-of-it Ed Chemical Brother and donated/abandoned the Winnebago to several other friends. Then, with clever positioning, my 'girlfriend' and I managed to hitch a lift onto Pulp's tour bus over to Babington House, where some of the band were also staying.

At Babington, everyone checked in, and before too long we were all congregating around the bar in the main house. Jarvis seemed to be particularly interested in my 'girlfriend', but that may have been because he initially thought she was Chloë Sevigny, an actress who, funnily enough, I also fancied but was also not going out with at the time.*

That night, the post-Glastonbury euphoria gave way to exhaustion, and the band slowly disappeared to their rooms. My soon-to-be ex non-girlfriend also decided to go to bed, and I suddenly realised that there were only three people left in the bar: myself, Jarvis, and his bodyguard, Colin.

I'd met Jarvis's bodyguard on many occasions previously, since he also worked with Suede and had looked after Noel and Liam Gallagher's security arrangements for several years. Colin had been kind enough to wave me through the various VIP rope barriers I'd encountered on my travels—first rule of rock'n'roll PR: get to

---

* The following year, I would get a well-deserved comeuppance for my misdiagnosis of the boyfriend/girlfriend scenario when I brought the same close friend—who was a girl (keep up!)—to Glastonbury only for her to sleep with a guy (she already knew) in the tent we'd put up together.

'I don't know who I am anymore,' I said, when we bumped into each other at some point during the weekend.

She could have said, 'I do. You're not my boyfriend.' But instead she said, 'Then stop taking drugs.'

Which was easy for her to say.

At Babington House back in June 1998, mind you, this was a future nightmare yet to reveal itself.

know the security—and I liked him a great deal. Still, it seemed most unusual to encounter him in the countryside. It was like bumping into your mum at a Throbbing Gristle gig.

Colin, Jarvis, and I removed ourselves to the front steps of the house so that Jarvis and I could share a cigarette by the front door. It must have been getting on for 4am when I decided it would be a good idea to chop some lines out on the impressive stone step beneath our feet.

'Look,' I think I said. 'It's completely flat. It's a very easy thing to do. Colin, would you have one?'

'No way, Phill,' said Colin. 'Not whilst I am working. And, anyway, you never know who is watching.'

'What do you mean?' I replied. 'We're in the middle of Somerset. Who could possibly be watching us round here?'

Colin thought for a moment.

'You just never know,' he said.

Jarvis and I exchanged a look, and then all three of us shared a conversation about the chances that we were being observed by a third party—like God being there to experience a tree fall in the wood, whilst no one is around to hear it—at all times of the day or night. I think Colin enjoyed the irony, but it was hard to tell.

Colin eventually consented to Jarvis and me being allowed to leave his protection—although perhaps he hadn't counted on the chances that Jarvis might take the opportunity to murder his PR for wearing heavy slap and earrings—so we were allowed to abandon the coke idea and explore the Babington grounds together. It was almost light when we stumbled upon a collection of parked cars that didn't seem to be in proper working order. Jarvis leapt on one and walked around on the roof and bonnet whilst I wondered whether to join him. After a while, however, I could tell that Jarvis was beginning to feel guilty that he might be damaging a real car that belonged to a real person. He jumped off before I could make a decision either way. An enduring image of the evening remains: a very tall man standing bolt upright on the roof of a Hillman Imp.

The next morning, my never-was-my girlfriend and I returned to London, and normal service was resumed—for me, at least. For Babington House it was another story, as that very same morning it was raided by the police and immigration authorities due to the assumption that eleven Polish immigrants had been working there illegally. Apparently the raid had involved most of them being chased across the grounds and surrounding fields by men in helicopters. It was strange to think that Colin had been right all along: we were being watched at all times of the day and night.

The Babington incident was indicative of a wider malaise, however—to whit, my relationship with Jarvis had always been on rocky ground. When Savage & Best first signed Pulp, it was mainly due to Lush's Miki Berenyi—John Best's girlfriend at the time—being obsessed with the band, telling John that they'd suddenly become rather good, after many years in the wilderness, and that we should do their press. So they'd always felt like John's band. Much later, when Melissa (from Savage & Best) was looking after their PR more than I was, it felt like I was regularly associated with their most awkward moments. When their album *This Is Hardcore* was released in March 1998, it came complete with a Peter Saville–directed cover photo by John Currin, best known for his figurative paintings of exaggerated female forms, which were digitally manipulated by Howard Wakefield; the subsequent media storm resulted in posters for the album on the London Underground system being defaced with graffiti stating *This Offends Women*, *This Is Sexist*, and *This Is Demeaning*, and who should have to get up at 6am one morning to defend the artwork? Well, yours truly, that's who, and don't think it was easy fending off several prearranged interrogations by some of the finest women's organisations in the country.

Some months earlier, I'd driven Jarvis to Holland Park—in my *gleaming, antique Porsche*—to complete a fairly routine *Melody Maker* cover photo session, only to be confronted on the park's perimeter by a parks official, who insisted we have the correct insurance documents to take photographs. Cue several phone calls to Island Records and their lawyers, a fee of one million pounds being discussed, and the photo session subsequently taking place elsewhere. And then there was the press fuss surrounding *This Is Hardcore* itself. 'Death, Porn, Heroin—What's Eating Jarvis Cocker?' spat the cover of the April 1998 issue of *Select* magazine, and you can bet I was blamed for the magazine's take on the subject. 'The rumour persists that Pulp and heroin are no strangers,' Jarvis was offered by means of a question at the time, but when the magazine asked me if I knew whether the band actually took heroin—and I can't believe I was asked this question either—I just said, 'I don't know—"The Fear"'s about drugs, but the album's called *This Is Hardcore*, why don't you just read the lyrics?' Naturally, my vague off-hander became parlance for *there's more to this than meets the eye*, and Pulp were condemned forthwith. But Jarvis surely added fuel to the fire. 'One thing I will say about it is this,' he said in reply. 'I think that what happens is, say, you've got a group of ten people who're friends and they all do that kind of thing, everybody eggs everybody else on, but if you talked to each individual person out of that group and said, *Are you really wanting to do that?* they'd probably say, *No, I think I'd be better off without*. It's peer pressure. Like when your mum says to you, *If Martin Hunt jumped in some dog dirt, would you?* The answer is probably, *Yeah, I would. If he said it were a good laugh, yeah, I'd do it.*' Which didn't really help.

And then there was the Action Man party.

One early evening in 1996, Jarvis was hanging round in the office after an interview, and one of us suggested that we should go to a party around the corner before heading off into the night. Unfortunately, the party was an Action Man 30th Anniversary Party—not something you would even think of attending without the possibility of free sex and drugs—but attend it we did nonetheless. Jarvis has subsequently claimed that he only went to the party because Pulp bandmate Russell Senior would meet him there, but I can't see why Russell would have even considered

176

attending an event like this. No, I can only surmise that Jarvis agreed to go this party because he had nothing better to do and he felt sorry for me.

When Jarvis and I arrived at the party, I'd rarely received such affection.

'Oh, my God, Phill!' gushed the celebrity PR Mark Borkowski, who was representing Action Man—what a soulful requisition that was—and hosting the Action Man party that evening. 'I can't believe you brought Jarvis with you. This is amazing. This makes the whole event worthwhile. I can't thank you enough.'

He may as well have said, 'I can't believe I've genuinely earned my fees from a client for the first time ever.'

Extraordinarily enough, Borkowski's incumbent staff were even more keen to embrace Jarvis's attendance, ushering him to have his picture taken with *The Man* himself at every juncture. I recoiled with embarrassment, but when asked whether there was a moment he thought his 'going out' had got out of control, Jarvis sums up this awful experience much better than I ever could: 'Probably when I found myself shaking hands with Action Man [*looks shame-faced*] at a party for Action Man's thirtieth birthday. That was the moment I really thought, *You should consider staying at home for a bit.* Action Man had gripping hands though. And eagle eyes.'

Things got worse. The photographs of Jarvis and Action Man were distributed throughout the tabloid media—Borkowski's henchmen and women had done their job—and Jarvis had suddenly become a laughing stock. *The Sun* was particularly vicious in its condemnation—Jarvis remembers 'fucking Andy Coulson saying, *If you see Jarvis out at a lig, ring us up and we'll give you a tenner*, and all this shit'—and I remember one particular headline about Jarvis offering his services to attend 'the opening of an envelope' making me feel suitably mortified. Indeed, it was around this time—or maybe it was around every time that I was in Jarvis's presence—that I felt something was amiss. Pulp may have had a uniquely symbiotic relationship with audience and fan alike, but I felt there was one going on closer to home—namely between their defiantly unravelled singer and his PR.

CHAPTER 10

YOU'RE IN
THE ART
WORLD NOW

"Fifteen grand! I think. I've never
even seen fifteen grand before, let
alone been given it. If I can just get
this bag back to my house without
anyone knowing about it, then the
office needn't know anything about
it either."

'Can I introduce you please / To a lump of Cheddar cheese.'
—Fat Les, 'Vindaloo', 1998.

Believe it or not, back in the early throes of May 1998, with World
Cup fever a distant dream away, there were only two songs pop
pundits could ever envisage getting anywhere near the top of the
charts. One was the 'official', Football Association–endorsed, Ian
McCulloch–penned '(How Does It Feel To Be) On Top Of The
World'—performed by Echo & The Bunnymen, Ocean Colour
Scene, Space, and The Spice Girls—and the other was the much-
fancied re-release of Baddiel & Skinner's 'Three Lions'. Rumour
has it that the race between these two was so well orchestrated
that the heads of their respective record companies had agreed
on a deal where the records would be released in alternate weeks.
Who could have envisaged that an as-yet-unrecorded song called
'Vindaloo' would go on to sell a million copies and casually
marauder on to be the twenty-fourth bestselling single of the year
(ahead of Robbie Williams's 'Angels')? And who would have bet
money on a follow-up single—the fabulously ludicrous and saucy
'Naughty Christmas'—spending four weeks in the Top 40 and
selling seventy-five thousand copies in the process? Not Radio 1,
for a kick off, who played 'Vindaloo' and 'Naughty Christmas' a
grand total of two times each before their releases. But myself and
the press—well, herein lies a tale.

In April 1998, I had a telephone call from Blur's Alex James.

'There's someone I'd like you to meet,' he said. 'It's Keith Allen.

Do you know him? Anyway, we've written a World Cup song together, and I want you to do the press for it.'

I'd known Alex for several years, ever since he'd made a point of tracking me down as he was jealous (on behalf of Blur) of all the press Suede were getting. Damon was jealous, too, but Alex was less precious than his counterpart—and even less inhibited, due to his alcohol intake—but it's also true to say that I knew Alex through Polly in our office, who was much closer than I was to either of them, having spent the first few years of her career working for Blur's record label, Food Records, which was housed next door. When we poached her from Food, I boasted that all she'd had to do was wander across the rooftop into our first floor Camden office on Arlington Road. And still, when she joined Savage & Best, and Food was but a distant memory, Damon would ring her and ask, 'What are Suede up to?'

Two years earlier, Alex had been part of Me Me Me, the Britpop 'supergroup' who'd further comprised Elastica's Justin Welch and Stephen Duffy, previously of The Lilac Time. Both were Savage & Best artists, and when their only single, 'Hanging Around', released in August 1996, reached the UK Top 20 after an inordinate amount of press attention (largely due to Rachel in our office), Alex must have thought we could make anything successful. Henceforth, after he and Keith came up with the rhythmic pop musings that were later to become 'Vindaloo'— after spending the afternoon at Ashton Gate, watching Bristol City against Fulham—his thoughts must have turned to Savage

181

& Best and the possibility of having a much bigger hit.

But anyway, I knew exactly who Keith Allen was: after all, I'd been a student in the 1980s (not, as some people have suggested, a student *of* the 1980s who listens to Absolute 80s as a matter of course and thinks the works of Soft Cell and Tears For Fears are as important as the Renaissance—that would be ridiculous), and there wasn't a member of that cruelly, culturally, socially neglected group that hadn't seen every single episode of *The Comic Strip Presents*. Indeed, the episode where Keith Allen stars as 'The Yob'—about a pretentious promo director somehow getting his brain switched with that of a football hooligan after a psychic teleportation experiment goes wrong … with hilarious consequences—was a university staple. Every student digs boasted a VHS copy. I was intrigued.

Alex and I arranged to meet at the Groucho the following evening, but when I arrived there was no sign of him or his entourage. I mentioned to the concierge that I was hoping to meet Keith and Alex and received a look of such pity and disdain that I wondered if they'd been arrested for peddling filth earlier that day. I'd looked in every room before I got a tap on the shoulder.

'Hi Phill,' said Alex. 'Guys, this is Phill Savidge, the guy I told you about.'

Alex and I hug, and then I notice that there are three guys staring at me. One of them I recognise as Keith, and another is laughing. I'm pretty sure the latter is Damien Hirst.

Keith walks over to me and shakes my hand.

'So you're Phill, are you?' he says, pursing his lips and sounding not unlike a camper version of Kenneth Williams. 'I've heard a lot about you.'

At the time, I don't know what to make of this initial encounter, but it later transpires that Alex has told Keith and Damien that they shouldn't be surprised if he introduces them to someone who looks like a girl. Keith and Damien are genuinely surprised, however, and it takes some time for equilibrium to resume.

The third guy staring at me starts to set up the snooker table. His name is Jan Kennedy and he is either Damien's manager or agent, although the jury is out on the true nature of his vocation. He and Damien play a frame of snooker, and then it's my turn to play Keith. I beat him and he seems surprised. Alex looks on in amusement.

At some point, as the drugs and cocktails start to flow, Damien walks over to me and says, 'What do you reckon you can do for us?'

'Get you in the *NME* and *Melody Maker* every week and in the tabloids every day,' I say, somewhat disingenuously.

'Great,' says Damien, and he walks over to a chair where he had placed his rucksack after walking in. He pulls out a carrier bag and thrusts it into my arms.

'There's fifteen grand,' he says. 'You're hired.'

Keith and Alex start laughing, and it's only Jan who looks concerned.

I take a seat on a sofa and watch Alex and Damien playing

snooker. Everything appears normal, but all I can think about is the plastic bag, which I've placed at my feet.

Fifteen grand! I think. *I've never even seen fifteen grand before, let alone been given it. If I can just get this bag back to my house without anyone knowing about it, then the office needn't know anything about it either.*

At the very point when I am imagining what I can buy with my newfound wealth, Jan walks over and sits next to me on the sofa.

'Damien got that money from selling a sketch earlier today,' he says. 'You should give it back to him. He'll respect you much more in the morning.'

My heart sinks. What am I supposed to do now? I was expecting a simple business meeting.

Jan leaves the room and Keith comes over.

'What was he saying?' he asks.

'He said I should give the money back to Damien, 'cos he'll respect me if I do.'

'And what d'you think?' says Keith, laughing.

'I don't know,' I say.

Ten minutes later, when there is a break in the ongoing snooker tournament, I hand the bag back to Damien.

'You should have this back,' I say. 'We should sort out a proper monthly contract through your office and mine.'

Damien takes the bag off me and throws it into a corner. It appears to land next to two other bags each containing fifteen thousand pounds.

As I leave, Alex passes me a cassette. It's a small consolation.

The next day—and I have to confess it was early afternoon before I managed to make it in—the first thing I do when I arrive in the office is to tell everyone we're going to be doing PR for a football record that Keith and Alex have written and recorded. They all seem genuinely excited—particularly Rachel and Polly, who have always wanted to do something to take them away from the humdrum of music PR. (Or is that just me? I get confused sometimes.) I then produce the cassette that Alex had handed to me the night before. I put it on the office stereo, and to my surprise it is actually quite listenable. In the same way that a book can be quite readable and a film can be quite watchable. I put it on again, and the chorus begins to hit the nerve that it was always meant to hit, and I can't stop singing along. When I put it on for a third time, I am beginning to understand how effective the record is and where I am going to be spending the next three months. Polly and Rachel are laughing, as they no doubt think what I am thinking: this is nonsense of such a terrific order that it's going to be a massive success.

I ring Alex and tell him that the cassette he gave me contained the finest recordings known to humanity, and we laugh because he doesn't know whether I am joking or not. I suggest that we need to get some photographs of the 'band', and it is then that Alex mentions that there's been some kind of hitch: Damon has got wind of the project and doesn't want Alex putting his head above the parapet for any musical venture other than Blur. Which begs the question: has Damon actually heard the record? Because

185

musical is stretching it a bit. Anyway, it's going to have to be Keith and Damien that front Fat Les for the time being.

I agree that this is the best course of action, and my next call is to the photographer Donald Milne, who agrees to take some pictures of Keith and Damien the next day. I then call Keith and tell him that he has to be in Soho for nine the following morning. He suggests that I should meet him and Damien at the Groucho that night to discuss the campaign.

At the Groucho, I manage to grab a few lines off Keith whilst we're playing snooker. Damien is there, too, but he appears to be talking to so many people that it is impossible to get a word in edgeways. Keith and I talk about England winning the World Cup—we have been drawn against Tunisia, Columbia, and Romania for the group stages, and this seems an easy group to get out of. We also discuss our mutual love of golf and arrange to play the following week. At no point do we discuss the campaign, and at midnight, when I leave, Keith promises that he and Damien will be ready for their photo session at 9am the next day.

The following morning, I am on my way to the office when I get a call from Donald Milne.

'Where's Keith and Damien?' he asks. 'I've been here for an hour and there's no sign of them.'

I check my watch and it is after ten o'clock.

'Leave it with me,' I say.

I call Keith, and the deranged lunatic who is now in possession of his phone shouts down the line.

'Aarrgghh!'

'Keith,' I say calmly. 'Why the fuck aren't you at the photo session? Where are you?'

'We're still at the Groucho,' shouts Keith. 'Ha, ha, ha, ha! Here, have a word with Damien.' There is a muffled sound of a phone being handed over a table full of drinks or snooker balls.

'Hello,' says Damien. 'What d'you want?'

'You're over an hour late for the photos, and we need them by this afternoon,' I yell. 'If you don't do them, I can't get any press.'

There is a pause whilst Damien digests the information.

'That's music bollocks,' he shouts. 'This is different. You're in the art world now.'

Somehow, given the opposition presented by The Terrible Twins, Donald manages to produce some new photographs, and, together with pictures of buckets of vindaloo shot by Damien earlier, I contrive to get some kind of press campaign under way. I tableau a few key phrases in my head—*a postmodern salute to multiculturalism* was one, *a gay football anthem for children* was another, and *a thin line between stupid and clever* was the cream of the crop—and it's not long before I have created some kind of phenomenon. *The Guardian* runs a big news story next to a photo of a bucket of vindaloo, the *Evening Standard* and *NME* do similar, and I am hard pushed to prevent *Elle* and *Esquire* running spreads on a single that they have no right to be interested in. Even John Harris, the newly incumbent editor of *Select*—and a serious journalist usually averse to triviality when it comes to all

187

matters music—is transfixed by the song and writes two pages on the subject for the magazine.

Of course, I know I can pull in trendy press till the vaches come home, but I also know that I owe it to Keith to make the record as populist as possible. I call Dominic Mohan at *The Sun*, and he agrees to run a double-page spread under the banner headline 'Let's Go Vindaloony', together with the lyrics, a competition, and a phone line to hear the song. The next day's edition carries a cartoon featuring a man trying to buy the record in a shop whilst being offered six free onion bhajis with his copy. Eighteen days before release, we have suddenly become part of the zeitgeist. It is time to have some fun.

It's around this time I manage to get Dominic down to *Top Of The Pops* so that he can feature in the pre-recorded video that will get shown if the record is ever a hit. We have almost been here before, but The Spice Girls were a distant memory when, just two days before release, the *Guardian Weekend* magazine pulls off the most ludicrously eye-catching, hilarious, and significant cover of the year. Fat Les look absurd, the article by cultural football commentator and author Kevin Sampson is a godsend and belongs in *Pseuds Corner*, and at the top of the page, in bold, the record is described as a 'postmodern tribute to multiculturalism'. Yes, you've guessed it: Alex James, drunk as a fish and dressed in bra, knickers, and wellies, has stolen my catchphrase and got it wrong.

Much to my surprise—and to the rest of the walking, talking, non-simian populace—'Vindaloo' goes in at no.2 in the charts and stays there for several weeks. In fact, the only event that prevents it becoming the biggest selling single of all time, and more revered and successful than 'Bohemian Rhapsody' or the 1997 version of 'Candle In The Wind' (is there any other version?), is England's expulsion from the World Cup after losing on penalties to Argentina in the sixteen. Keith and I were right all along: England's progress from the group stages—apart from a 2–1 loss to Romania—was simple enough. But eviction is eviction, and no one is going to buy an England World Cup football anthem—and I think we can say that 'Vindaloo' was an anthem by this point— when there's nothing to believe in anymore.

Does this sound overdramatic? Well, it was like that in those days: when the England football team got knocked out, life was over.

Eventually, however, life moved on, and two years after the runaway triumph of 'Vindaloo', the Football Association, having had its noses rubbed in it, decides to embrace Fat Les and officially endorse their version of 'Jerusalem'. The promotional budget was £50,000, which is absurd for a single even then—I mean to say, this was a good time after the excesses of the 1980s, and record companies had begun to calm down—but most amusing of all are Keith's negotiations with the FA over the video: initial copies feature Keith flying a Spitfire over what looks like Germany, but even an offer to paint-shop the Spitfire pink doesn't placate the FA, whose chiefs are afraid of being accused of promoting jingoism. Unsurprisingly, the official video ends up occupying a space somewhere between sombre and joyous, the orchestra and choirs at George Martin's Air Studios intermingling uneasily with the hotchpotch of cameos on offer. This time there are two Blurs (Alex again, and drummer Dave Rowntree) on offer; English planetary scientist Colin Pillinger, who's recently been befriended by Blur during the British *Beagle 2* Mars lander project; plus Alfie Allen, Danny Dyer, and the usual crop of likely suspects. One of these is Michael Barrymore.

The presence of Barrymore in the 'Jerusalem' project is entirely down to the fact that Keith has, for the last two months, been filming a sitcom series with Barrymore called *Bob Martin*. In *Bob Martin*, Barrymore plays a troubled daytime game-show host who is wiling to do anything he needs to get what he wants. It has a brilliant cast, including Dennis Lawson, Jamie Theakston, and Allen, and several famous people playing themselves (Anthea Turner, Paul Ross, Michael Aspel, Bob Mills, and Jeff Pope—the latter pair actually wrote the series), but the show is most notable for the fact that it's surely a less-realised version of *Extras*, which didn't turn up on our screens until five years later. (Well, that and perhaps *The Larry Sanders Show*.) For me, however, it was Barrymore's behaviour, and his appearance as the larger-than-life game-show host—both in reality and in the show itself—that made me wonder why he'd bothered to tack himself along to 'Jerusalem'.

Barrymore seemed self-obsessed and paranoid, inhabiting a netherworld somewhere between his onscreen persona and his *Bob Martin* character. Each time we met, he was carrying a bottle of red wine in his coat pocket, and occasionally he would take a surreptitious swig from the bottle as if he was being watched, the bottle liable to be confiscated at any moment. One day, we were playing golf at a very exclusive golf club, and I noticed that he'd transferred his bottle from his coat to his extremely expensive Calloway golf bag. Mind you, it wasn't just his bag that was expensive: he had a complete set of Calloway irons and woods that appeared not to have been used. When we teed off, however, I noticed that he used a seven iron, even though we were tackling a par four. Subsequently, he proceeded to use a seven iron for every shot throughout the entire round, as if he was frightened that any other club would show him up as a poor golfer—not realising, of course, that the use of a seven iron on every hole was demonstration enough.

I was in a four-ball with Barrymore, playing against Keith and fellow actor Kieran O'Brien, when I realised that the latter pair's constant ribbing of their opponents was wasted on him. O'Brien and Allen could, in some respects, survive quite happily as a vaudeville act, and their usual bullying of me often resulted in a missed putt here or a sliced drive there, but Barrymore proved to be slim pickings; he only seemed interested in talking about the dwindling audience figures for shows he hadn't been involved in, cracking the most outlandish, unrepeatable jokes, or marching down the fairway like John Cleese annoying the Germans in that episode of *Fawlty Towers*. When we finally finished the round we made the usual prevarications as to who had the drugs, and it turned out he had been 'holding' all along. I drew the long straw and soon found myself hunched over a sink in the disabled toilet of the clubhouse whilst Barrymore racked out several large lines. His cocaine was wet, yellow, and rubbish, although I still indulged—I'm not a complete fool—yet my overriding memory of the episode was when a loud knock at the cubicle door made me acutely aware that I was hiding in a toilet with Michael Barrymore.

'Is that Michael Barrymore in there?' said a voice. 'Michael Barrymore? Are you gay?'

For a moment, I thought Keith or Kieran were trying to freak us out, but then I realised it had been the voice of a child. Barrymore seemed somewhat unperturbed, taking one last snort of coke and marching towards the door. I followed quickly behind, and when we both emerged into the hallway of the clubhouse, I noticed about seven or eight children staring at us.

'It is! It's Michael Barrymore!' said one of the children, who couldn't have been more than twelve years old.

'Is it true that you're gay?' the boy asked again, and one or two of the children started sniggering.

'He can't be,' said another. 'Look, he's been in the toilet with a girl!'

Barrymore looked around in some confusion before deciding on a course of action.

'Now, move along children,' he said, in a manner not unlike the way his successful television persona might have dealt with a situation like this. 'There's nothing to see here.'

Barrymore then started to stride towards the children, and it was then I noticed a man standing at the entrance to the bar.

'Oi!' he shouted. 'I told you to leave him alone.'

The children immediately became downcast as if in disgrace, and Barrymore was almost upon them—in the nicest possible way—when I heard the man say, 'I'm sorry about that, Michael. But you know what they say: *Kids. Say. The. Funniest. Things!* Eh!'

Barrymore didn't reply—indeed, what was he meant to say?—and I wondered whether this was the kind of thing that happened to Michael Barrymore every day of his life. My other thought was: perhaps this is not such a posh golf club after all.

* * *

On June 17 2000, England were due to play Germany at the Stade du Pays in Charleroi, Belgium, in the group stages of the European Championships. I was particularly excited, since England had not beaten Germany in a competitive match since 1966, and the last time we'd come anywhere close, in 1970, I'd been sent to bed at half time for being six years old.* I was

---

* I was too young to remember England winning the World Cup, so my first memory of the competition is England playing West Germany in the quarter-finals in Mexico in 1970. We were two up at half time, and with a semi-final slot virtually guaranteed, my father looked at his watch, saw that it was late (the six-hour time difference meant it was well past my bedtime), and sent me to bed.

'Son,' he said. 'You should get some sleep. Don't worry; we've got this sewn up.'

If you don't want to know what happened next then look away now—I went to bed and the Germans won 3–2, with Gerd Muller slipping the ball past Peter Bonetti in extra time—but that particular episode has stuck with me my whole life.

not, however, particularly excited about the possibility of being chauffeured to the game in a small private plane flown by Alex James of the rock band Fat Les … I mean, Blur. Alex was known to have been awarded a licence to fly planes, but did this really mean he could fly a plane? I hated flying so much I used to make sure I never actually saw the metal contraption we were supposed to be flying in at any point, in order that I would never have to think about the logical impossibility of flight. But with an impending walk-the-plank sojourn to a tiny, four-seater aircraft in the offing, what was I supposed to do?

Keith's car picks me up from my Crouch End apartment early on Saturday morning, and I am presumably incensed that I have not been allowed to find my own way to Elstree Aerodrome. Still, when we arrive, I am surprised to find Alex and Barrymore already in residence and waiting in a seated wooden or tarpaulin area (it is hard to be exact about these things when the structure is so hideous) that can only be described as a waiting/seating area. This, presumably, is a clubhouse of sorts, and the acceptable face of private air travel.

I am introduced to an erstwhile BA pilot called Tony who, it transpires, I have met on several occasions at the Groucho club. He will be accompanying us on the trip to Charleroi, just in case Alex decides that he can't actually fly us the whole way there. We file into the plane one by one, and I am genuinely astonished when Alex manages to squeeze into the cockpit and press the appropriate buttons so that some kind of take-off is imaginable. Seconds later, we are laughing, as Hertfordshire and the outskirts of north London disappear beneath us.

Having said that, the most notable point about the entire journey is the tin-can nature of our passage over the White Cliffs of Dover: I admit, it's hardly Major Tom stuff, but when you never expected to be transported any higher than a trampoline would allow—other than during commercial aerospace travel—then it was stupidly enjoyable, particularly as, at this point, we had decided to enjoy the en-suite facilities provided. We crept about in our makeshift drug den, drinking and smoking and occasionally gazing at the cliffs, the English Channel, and ourselves. And, as France seamlessly morphed into Belgium, Alex gingerly stepped out of the cockpit, and Tony took over.

At Charleroi airport we were ushered into some kind of aircraft hanger—or was it a warehouse recently vacated by ravers?—where we were offered gin and tonics. We handed over our passports to an official who told us we were not the only English people flying in for the game: Mick Jagger and Elton John were due in at any moment. Twenty minutes later, when the man returned with our passports, he shouted out our titles and surnames—there was the usual confusion when he read out my details—so that we could each step forward. When it came to Barrymore's passport, there was even more confusion.

'Parker?' barked the official. No one budged.

'Parker,' he repeated, and this time Barrymore came forward to claim his passport.

'Parker?' said Keith. 'What's that all about?'

'Oh, you know,' said Barrymore. 'That's just the name I was born with.'

Keith and Alex nodded in rare sympathy, but you can bet that *Parker* became the put down of choice for the next few hours. I didn't have the heart to join in, figuring that I would soon be the object of further merriment when the appropriate moment arose.

Once the passports had been distributed, we climbed into a car and were taken into the town of Charleroi. The driver dropped us off as close to the stadium as possible, although we appeared to be in the middle of a melee of England supporters making their way on foot. Some of the crowd recognised Keith and started singing 'Vindaloo', and I noted with some regret that 'Jerusalem' was absent from their repertoire.

Barrymore was wearing a baseball cap that he'd turned around the wrong way, presumably so he wouldn't be recognised; either that or he was considering an ill-advised move into the world of hip-hop. Whatever the reason, the ploy was unsuccessful, and it wasn't long before the crowd latched on to the fact that the most famous game-show host in the UK was hiding amongst them. Barrymore had not been to a football match before—never mind one as vital as England versus Germany—and when the crowd starting chanting 'Awight!' he seemed scared and bemused.

At the stadium, which had the strangest, steepest incline of any ground I'd ever been to, we climbed to the top and hid amongst the genuine England fans who'd travelled from Sheffield,

Stoke, and Sunderland. No one took any notice of the odd little foursome embedded in their midst. When Alan Shearer scored the only goal, our section went crazy, and Keith, Alex, and I all hugged each other. I glanced around to see what Barrymore was up to and noticed he was still wearing his baseball cap turned back to front, sitting down, staring blankly ahead. He looked like the loneliest man in the world.

On the flight back to England, our hangovers were progressing nicely when someone suggested we play poker. Tony was permanently on flying duties at this point, and when the cards were dealt I realised that I hardly knew how to play. As I began to sober up, I also realised that I was now playing poker with three men who had much easier access to a million pounds than I did. I pretended to go to sleep, and when I woke up we had landed.

Back at Elstree Aerodrome, word had got around that Michael Barrymore had flown from the airport that morning, and presumably would be returning—well, about now actually. It was hardly The Beatles returning to Britain after their first US tour in 1964, but the first five minutes were spent watching Barrymore sign autographs and ordering a car to take us back into town. An hour later, we were all back at the Groucho, playing snooker and watching telly, when the opening bars of the *Match Of The Day* theme tune heralded an unprecedented chant of our own:

'We were there!'

I'm not sure if anyone believed us.

Three days later, I drove back to Charleroi without the Fat

Lezzers—and how many times has Keith wanted the band to be referred to in this way?—to see England face Romania in the last game in the group stages. The experience could not have been more contrasting: I met a Sunderland fan who had cycled to the stadium from the North East but been refused entry to the stadium due to his huge intake of alcohol; despite England being 2–1 ahead at half time, the right-footed Phil Neville proved such an inept left back that he gifted a penalty to Romania in the last few minutes and ensured England never reached the quarter-finals; and I contracted food poisoning, ensuring that the drive back to England was utterly miserable. It was miserable for another reason, too. With England out of the Euros, it was the end of 'Jerusalem'—and, perhaps, the end of Fat Les.

* * *

In 2004, as a long-time Fulham fan, Keith Allen recorded 'We're Not Real Madrid' as Colin & The Cottagers, and Fulham FC's then owner, Mohamed Al Fayed, was impressed enough to arrange for Keith and me to stay at the Ritz in Paris for a weekend as some kind of reward. The song 'What Have I Done To Deserve This?' immediately sprang to mind, but after travelling on the Friday Eurostar to Paris and checking in at the hotel, we both noticed that the front desk and concierge kept exchanging glances and whispering *Friends of Mohamed*. When the initial commotion had died down, we were escorted to a suite, which, we were assured, was the same suite shared by Diana and Dodi seven years earlier, on the night of their deaths—although I am almost certain it was at least twice as big, with several more bathrooms. As I lounged around in my own enormous section of the suite, dressed in my salmon-pink Ritz dressing gown, glancing occasionally at my complimentary Ritz wristwatch, I could hear the muffled sounds of Keith shouting as loud as he could from his own part of the suite which, if not in the same time zone, was certainly reachable by a small space rocket within several light years.

'Do you want an E?' shouted Keith in an unnecessarily deafening tone, and even though I said yes it is possible that Keith didn't receive my answer for at least two centuries.

'We have tickets for the Paris Saint-Germain game tomorrow,' he continued. 'And if you don't want to get into trouble, you should take that watch off. There are cameras everywhere, and we don't need to look like we're on the payroll.'

Keith and I then had a discussion about the ongoing *cash for questions* scandal, and the fact that the Conservative politician Neil Hamilton, and several others, had recently been questioned for accepting gifts during their stays at the Ritz hotel. We agreed that it was best to ditch the watches and continue to wear our salmon-pink dressing gowns.

From that point onwards, the weekend got out of hand: after we'd both consumed an E, we ventured downstairs, but as Keith was still wearing his complimentary Ritz salmon pink-dressing gown, and complimentary Ritz salmon-pink slippers—I had changed into a much more fashionable outfit—whilst smoking a giant Cuban cigar, our appearance in the main dining room was not without controversy. We were subsequently moved from room to room whilst bar staff and the rest of the hotel employees considered whether we should be escorted from the hotel or lauded for being *Friends of Mohamed*. Eventually, the events of the evening proved tiresome enough for all concerned, and we grabbed a car to take us across town.

The plan was to visit the Israeli-born French actor and director Yvan Attal—who was currently shooting a movie featuring Keith, Terence Stamp, and Yvan's long-term girlfriend, Charlotte Gainsbourg—at his apartment somewhere in Paris. On the way, Keith made several phone calls to the Complaints Department of the British Broadcasting Corporation.

'Is that the BBC Complaints Division?' he asked, in his campest Welsh voice. 'It is! Now, there's lovely. Except I've got a terrible complaint about your output earlier this evening. I was watching *Blankety Blank* presented by Lily Savage, and my son and I both suddenly realised that Lily was a man wearing women's clothing. My son is now utterly traumatised by the episode. Can you tell me what you intend to do about this utterly appalling situation?'

Keith had his phone on loudspeaker, but there was a discernible pause from the BBC Complaints Division before a woman's voice said, 'Is that Keith Allen?'

At Yvan's typically stylish ground-floor Parisian apartment, we drank champagne and took some more ecstasy. Then, at around two o'clock in the morning, a beautiful girl who appeared to be about sixteen years old emerged from a side room clutching a baby. I couldn't work out how a girl so young could have given birth to a child—although I realise it's not that unusual in the grander scheme of things—before I realised that the *girl* was Charlotte Gainsbourg, a woman in her early thirties. She seemed not at all annoyed that we had knocked on her door in the middle of the night.

It got late—really late—and Charlotte, Keith, and I got a car back to the Ritz whilst Yvan stayed with the baby. At the hotel, Keith walked into the bar and was confronted by several Ritz employees who all insisted that he should be wearing a tie. They were just about to escort him off the premises when Charlotte, who'd been dawdling behind somewhat, appeared in the bar beside him and leapt into his arms, wrapping her legs round his torso. The waiters, instantly recognising Charlotte as one of the most famous actresses in the country, backed off immediately, and we were allowed to stay in the bar. I noticed several of the bar staff whispering to each other, *I told you: Friends of Mohamed.*

I don't remember much about the rest of the weekend except that when we made it back to our suite and turned on one of the televisions, Paris Saint-Germain were already halfway through their match. Twenty-four hours later, when we were checking out—minus the complimentary watches, but with our salmon-pink dressing gowns stuffed into our overnight bags—I detected a distinctly warmer attitude from the guys on the door: it was almost as if our small connection to true French film aristocracy had reached as far as the front desk. We were handed the bill, and there was a moment when we wondered whether there'd been a terrible mistake and we were actually culpable for the tens of thousands of euros detailed herein. But no, there were the friendly, exchanged glances again, and we were merrily bid on our way.

* * *

Five years later, I am promoting another Fat Les record called 'Who Invented Fish And Chips?' The lyrics run, '*Who invented Fish? God. Who invented Chips? God did too. Who invented Fish & Chips? The English did. Well who invented poo? The Dutch. No,*' although the true beauty of the song surely lies in the spoken bridge:

> *Fifty percent of the inventions inverted after the Second World War have been English. Trains, Boats, Planes, Computers, Penicillin, Connect Four, Countdown, Generation Game, Telephones, Parliament, National Health, Luddites, Bessemer Converter, Spinning Jenny, Steam, Internal Combustion, Hovercraft, The Clash, Blur, Oasis, Beatles, The Rolling Stones, Capstan Full Strength, Navy Rum, Hipsters, Hippies, Flares, Vera Lynn, and Chris Kamara.*

Whilst perhaps not 'Vindaloo' or 'Jerusalem', it is stirring stuff.

The song had actually been released before. In 2002, Lily and Alfie Allen, and Wayne Sleep the dancer, featured in the video, and Wayne himself agreed to dress up—along with Keith, Alex, and Damien—as a member of The Beatles for a cover of the *Times Magazine*, shot by David Bailey. (The idea is that they are renamed The Fattles—geddit—for these purposes, but no one really gets it, so it's quickly abandoned). I had met Bailey twice before—once when he shot Suede for the cover of the *Sunday Times Magazine* and had proceeded to refer to each member of the band as if they were members of The Rolling Stones (Simon was Charlie, Brett was Mick, you get the picture), and once when he'd shot Ultrasound and affectionately said to Tiny, 'You're a fucking fat fucker, aren't you!' Mind you, he wasn't so affectionate when Tiny sat down and nearly broke his sofa.

The *Times Magazine*'s superb article (written by Robert Crampton) notwithstanding, the 2002 version of 'Who Invented Fish And Chips?'—released to coincide with the World Cup in South Korea and Japan—is not a great success. However, there were high hopes for its re-release in 2010, with the main *Times* music correspondent, Will Hodgkinson, referring to it as 'a big, fat, pasty faced smash'. But no amount of cajoling and PR fun and games would persuade the rest of the media that we were still part of the zeitgeist. Either I had lost my touch or it was the end of an era. Or no doubt both.

By the time Fat Les became Fit Les to coincide with the 2012 London Olympics—the name was a nod to *the austere times we live in, the outfit having slimmed down after jettisoning previous partner-in-crime/ex-Blur cheese-maker Alex James for being too cheesy* (my rhetoric at the time)—the game was almost up. Fat Les were still *the million-selling anarchic pop-art collective fronted by maverick actor/comedian Keith Allen,* but even the song's deliberately provocative rebranding as 'The Official Fit Les Olympics Anthem' proved inconsequential. The *anthem* may have been a barbed comment on the corporatism surrounding that year's festivities, the inappropriateness of the countless sponsors involved (the only branded food was that of sponsors McDonald's, Coca-Cola, and Cadbury) and the fact that the original spirit of the Olympics had been forgotten, but no one took any notice.

Those Olympics prices in full:

Beer: £6 per pint

Coca-Cola-branded bottled water: £1.80

Cup of tea: £2.00

Cup of coffee £2.60

18.7cl bottle of wine: £4.80

There's a thin line between stupid and clever.

CHAPTER 11

SOME KIND OF METAL HAIR

"I'm wearing a blue agnès b. suit and sling-backs, I suggested. Oh, and I've got a Chihuahua on each shoulder."

By the time the 1990s came to an abrupt end, I was already planning my departure from the music business. This may have come as a shock to John and everyone else at Savage & Best, but it was something I'd been meaning to get around to for quite some time. About twelve years, to be exact. For the record, I'm still in it.

When the end of Savage & Best arrived, it was swift and, whilst not exactly painless, not altogether unlaced with humour, either; the lease on our sexy offices on Parkway in Camden was up for renewal, and I couldn't be bothered to look for new premises. John, ever the realist, had other ideas. He spent several weeks on the prowl, visiting potential new venues, but after I'd rejected the fifth one he'd found to show me, he began to lose his temper.

'You don't seem particularly interested,' he said, as we stood amongst the emptiness of a windowless building in Kentish Town. 'Why don't you like this one?'

'It's got no windows,' I pointed out, with remarkable accuracy. 'I can't work somewhere where there aren't any windows.'

John sighed.

'The last one was too dark,' he said, with ill-disguised irritation. 'And the one before that was too high up. And too office-y. Anyone would think you don't want to get new offices.'

'Well, I don't,' I said. 'I can't see what's wrong with the ones we've got now.'

John sighed again.

'Look, Phill,' he said. 'Maybe you and I should go our separate ways.'

206

'Maybe we should,' I replied.

And, with these three words, so ended the longest relationship I'd ever had.

The split was like a divorce. Except we'd never slept together. So exactly like a divorce. And we had to tell the children.

We called everyone into what passed for our meeting room and made the announcement. There was shock and then sadness, followed by swapped, nervous exchanges as each person in turn mentally manoeuvred into position.

In a quiet moment, I plucked up the courage to ask Rachel if she'd work with me in my new venture. Bravely, she agreed, even though I had very little idea what it was.

'I'll come with you on one condition,' she said. 'I'm not going to be your fucking secretary.'

Suede, Fat Les, Ultrasound, JJ72, The Auteurs, and Black Box Recorder—the latter was a Luke Haines offshoot, also featuring John Moore and Sarah Nixey, that brought Luke his only Top 20 hit with 'The Facts Of Life'—would also agree to join me, which sounds impressive until you realise that only two of these bands actually paid me any regular money. Pulp stayed with John because he rang them the minute we split up—surprise! I didn't ring anyone—and because they were always John's band, really. Each and every one of my erstwhile, beautiful office companions either moved on elsewhere or, like Polly, joined John—in his new venture. I couldn't blame them: he was a far more reliable prospect than someone who wouldn't move offices as they were too office-y, and who was still in the habit of going out on a Monday and coming back on a Thursday.

Saul Galpern at Nude Records offered me some office space with a W1 postcode, and I accepted, since this made me seem like I was moving up in the world. Subsequently, as I was walking with Saul past the advertising agency Saatchi & Saatchi on Charlotte Street, I realised what I should call my new company: I would call it Savage & Savidge. That way—in my most vivid dreams—some people might think that John had been sacked, and I'd replaced him with a relative. It would also keep the rhythm that the Savage & Best name engendered, and everyone else out there in the wider public marketplace—I'm only using this terminology since you expect me to—would assume we were a well-established agency with at least two partners.

It didn't quite work out like that. In fact, the first few enquiries we received asked whether Rachel and I had got married.

'No,' I replied.

So who's the other Savidge?'

'That's my brother,' I said, 'but he's an arse, and he's never in the office.'

John kept asking me the name of my new company, but I told him he'd have to read the following week's *Music Week* to find out. We'd both been interviewed separately when they'd heard about the break-up.

'You know you can't keep calling yourself Savage & Best?' he informed me, somewhat haughtily.

'Why the fuck would I want to keep calling myself Savage & Best?'

John shrugged.

On May 29 1999, *Music Week* put the Savage & Best split story on their cover, and John learned the name of my new company.

'Very funny,' he said.

I don't think he thought it was very funny. I think he thought it was very clever. But I also think he thought the whole episode was a little bit sad.

Music Week's story heralded the 'huge success' of Savage & Best, calling us 'a linchpin of independent music PR', next to a picture of John and me, looking suitably nonplussed. It felt like a big deal but no big deal. What *was* a big deal, however, was *Music Week*'s revelation that 'Savage & Savidge is looking to expand its interests into areas such as PR for footballers'.

That's a good one, I thought, and then, *Well it must be true, that's what I told them last week when they interviewed me! But footballers? What was I thinking of?* Just the thought of talking to them about music made me wince; they're the kind of breed whose idea of a good time is to outbid one another for tickets to see a secret show by Mariah Carey or Jamiroquai. I can only think that it must have been part of an ill-conceived plan to make me seem more impressive than I really was. And, perhaps, it would make Rachel think that we had a future together.

Rachel and I settled into our W1 postcode and stayed there until Nude Records folded the following year. We soon found another office, however, complete with real windows and an alternative W1 postcode, and we started a sideline photographic agency, headed up by a young friend of ours called Grace. Two further employees helped the office run, if not exactly smoothly, then, perhaps, sideways. One was called Tina, and I liked her because she was eccentric and glamorous and seemed to have all the right connections when it came to drugs and parties; and the other was Keith Allen's daughter, Lily, who spent most of her working day sitting on the floor rolling spliffs. *Fine by me*, I thought. *This is beginning to look like a proper office again.*

One day, I received a call from Darren Hughes, the hugely successful nightclub entrepreneur and co-founder of super-club Cream, whose Liverpool origins stretched back to October 1992. He said I'd been recommended to him as the right person to PR a massive project he'd been working on for some time. Would I be free to meet him and his business partner, Ron McCulloch, in Leicester Square to discuss the project? I said I would.

The meeting was to be held at 1 Leicester Square, an address I could only be envious of, but when I got there, I couldn't find the entrance. Eventually, when I found it, located down a side street, I was ushered into a silver/glass/steel/mirrored elevator—it was difficult to tell—and told to make my way to the sixth floor.

The building turned out to be the home of, ahem, Home nightclub, a 'super-club' that had opened its doors in September the previous year with much initial fanfare but little traction, after its inauguration onto the London club scene. The venture's failure to ignite the public's long-term interest had been hampered by the launch of Fabric, another super-club that had somehow managed to commandeer the cool common ground by opening one month later in Smithfield Market, thus ensuring it never had the ignominy of opening in the middle of the tourist hellhole that was central London. This, I surmised, must be the reason why I had never heard of Home in the first place. Or perhaps I'd just been reading the *NME* for so long I'd not been concentrating on anything that had been going on in the dance-music arena.

Which begs the question: was I the right person to represent the project in the first place? I mean, Savage & Best had represented Faithless, and I'd personally looked after the magnificent Fluke—one of the greatest techno bands of all time—both on and off Creation, and I'd spent many hours listening to obscure techno tunes at the insanely hip Pure club in Edinburgh, but doing PR for anything dance oriented was always going to be problematic. Just how much can you write about the joys of getting off your face and listening to dance music? (Guitarists, and indeed readers of *Guitar* and *Guitarist*, haven't we been here before?) And, often, you'd find the people behind the music were so uninspiring—glorified knob-twiddlers all, The Chemical Brothers excepted—that you'd have to spend twice as long explaining to journalists why they were really worth speaking to.

But this project felt somehow different.

I stepped out of the elevator on to the sixth floor and saw Darren and Ron immediately. This was hardly surprising, since they looked like the only people who would be literally mad enough to own—or lease—a place like this. The pair proved to be charming and scary in equal measure, and their charming scariness combined to agree on one thing: I would be retained to represent their Home venture.

And what a venture it was. We were sitting in an as-yet-not-fully realised private members' bar with a spectacular view over Leicester Square—and, indeed, most of London. You could see the London Eye and St Paul's Cathedral with very little difficulty, and it really was one of the most spectacular views I'd ever witnessed. Unsurprisingly, I learned the bar was to be called the View Bar.

My brief was impressively pompous: I would organise private parties in the View Bar on the sixth floor with a view to recruiting those who would want to pay to attend the club as private members on a regular basis; I would ensure that Home nightclub itself—actually located on the three floors below the View Bar— would receive positive press attention at all times; and I would invite people to dine with me—for lunch or for dinner—at Seven Restaurant on the seventh floor of the building, an establishment with a slightly better view of the London Eye and St Paul's Cathedral. And slightly better lobster.

Seven was a revelation—and not in a good way. Never had I encountered such a rich man's folly, such an excuse for extravagantly civilised, culinary activity. And it was not as if the food wasn't wonderful or the décor unimaginative, it was just that the concept was so spectacularly part of an afterthought that it never stood a chance. I was informed that I could dine for half price with *friends*—were they insane, didn't they realise I didn't have any friends?—in the restaurant, but if I dined with journalists, the meal would be gratis. Can you imagine, therefore, dear reader, how I decided to deal with this dreadful situation? Yes, you've guessed it: all my friends became journalists; Crispin from The Longpigs became the *Evening Standard*'s food critic, Rachel and Grace—the restaurant staff weren't to know—were reviewing the restaurant for their local newspaper; and several girlfriends were charmed when I introduced them to the concierge as food columnists for *The Observer* or *Time Out*. I ended up eating lobster every day for the next three months.

If you think the scenario associated with Seven was absurd, you should bear witness to proceedings at the View Bar. Naturally, I was awarded an unlimited drinks tab for friends and journalists—*hoorah*, I hear you cry—and I would often end an evening surrounded by twenty or thirty people, drinking sea breezes or mojitos whilst they congratulated me on my good fortune. It didn't really bother me that they were only there because of the free entertainment, since that was the only reason I was there in the first place. I like to think, however, they enjoyed the absurdity of the situation as much as I did.

Extraordinarily enough, I did manage to persuade several journalists to write about Seven, and I also procured a substantial amount of people to take temporary membership of the View Bar. Some of these even spent tens of thousands of pounds of their own money on their bar bills when I wasn't around to finance their proclivities. Darren and Ron seemed pleased, and it was suggested that I take *The Home Experience* to the next level. Although, as it transpired, there was to be no Level Eight.

Home, the nightclub, had been the elephant in the room all along, and I avoided visiting it—or *experiencing* it—for as long as I could. Eventually, however, it became more awkward to pretend I had to be in bed by 1am when my demeanour indicated that I had no intention of going to bed until the following evening. One Friday night, I bit the bullet and ventured downstairs to the club.

The club was situated on three floors—the third, fourth, and fifth floors of the building—although the dance floor itself was located on the third floor and the other two floors consisted of wraparound bars and viewing terraces. There was one thing that united all the floors, however, and that was the fact they were all virtually empty.

The music was excellent—and I knew that Paul Oakenfold, a resident DJ, was director of music policy, and that other DJs included Steve Lawler and Dave Haslam—but as there didn't seem to be that many people listening to it, its excellence was somewhat diminished. The few people that were there were later described to me as the *bridge-and-tunnel crowd*, which just about summed them up: out-of-towners who'd come to the West End looking for the high life. There didn't seem to be anything positive I could say about the venue.

The problems with Home stemmed from the fact that

Westminster Council's licensing laws meant that the club had been denied a 6am licence, thus ensuring that serious clubbers would avoid the place like the plague. This, coupled with the fact that its only super-club rival, Fabric, had been granted a 6am licence and was situated in a more desirable, urban environment, ensured that Home was never going to be a success.

But Home did have an ace up its sleeve: as part of the Home franchise, it was intimately connected to the seminal Space nightclub in Ibiza. What if I could use this exotic setting as leverage to promote its sister venue in Leicester Square? Indeed, couldn't it be said that the combination of Seven, the View Bar, Home nightclub, and Space in Ibiza would provide the ultimate, unique, twenty-four-hour clubbing experience?

I called Saffron from Republica—a good friend, and one of the artists we used to look after at Savage & Best—and asked her if she wanted to be involved in a piece about twenty-four-hour clubbing. She agreed, so I contacted the *Evening Standard*'s Tim Cooper and asked whether he'd be able to run a two-page story on Saffron's attempt to go twenty-four-hour clubbing. He thought it was a great idea. We arranged to meet the following Saturday at 9pm.

On the day in question, Saffron and I arrived at Home at nine o'clock and made our way to the seventh floor, where we dined magnificently—although neither of us ate anything. Tim Cooper soon joined us, and we swiftly progressed to the View Bar, where we drank cocktails until it was time to descend to the nightclub, so that a photographer could take pictures of Saffron dancing. Unsurprisingly, the club was not full, and our photo session caused very little fuss. At 2am, Saffron, Tim, and I climbed into a car and were whisked away to Gatwick Airport to meet the plane that was to take us to Ibiza.

As twenty-four-hour clubbing features go, Gatwick Airport was not a nice experience: as soon as we arrived, I got a nosebleed, and Saffron appearing to be suffering from nervous exhaustion. Tim, on the other hand, who'd not been indulging in anything other than the fine dining experience that was Seven, was—quite literally—full of beans and raring to go. He seemed to be amused by proceedings. Somehow, I managed to check in without attracting too much attention, although I admit I placed a blanket over my head as soon as I found my seat on the plane, refusing all offers of snacks and hot beverages.

In Ibiza, Saffron and I were driven to our hotel, where we were expected to share a room. This was news to both of us, but we laughed about it, changed our clothing, and headed off into the morning light. Outside the hotel, Tim and a guide—I hope you're laughing, Ibiza junkies, it sounds like we're in the jungle—joined us, and we made our way to the part of the island where Space was located. I don't know what I was expecting, but my initial impression was one of disappointment: the setting, the people, even the weather seemed to have been manufactured for my benefit.

But what did I expect? I was tired and emotional.

At the entrance to Space I was professional enough to make our introductions, and we were ushered through to a decked area on the outskirts of the main arena. I knew several people on the deck—the cast of *Is Harry On The Boat?* (including Keith Allen) were present, as the film was being shot in the area—and everyone seemed to be expecting us. There was an air of amused/bemused detachment. Someone handed me a large, vodka-based cocktail.

'Hello, you must be Phill,' said a voice, and I turned round to see a tanned individual wearing a white suit and a fedora, holding out his hand to shake mine. 'I work with Darren, and I've been told to look after you. He's over there.' The man pointed over in the direction of a group of people amongst whom I could see Darren looking suitably at home.

'Hi. Nice to meet you,' I said, shaking hands. 'This is Saffron and this is Tim,' I added, indicating my two partners in crime beside me.

We all chatted for several minutes, but it was in a distracted moment that the man in the fedora spoke quietly to me.

'Have you had a pill yet?' he asked gently.

'No, I said. 'Not yet. I'd love one though.'

'I'll get you some,' he said. 'Has the journo had one yet?'

'No,' I said. 'He doesn't take drugs.'

The effect of my words could not have been more profound: I may as well have revealed that the journalist was not a real journalist but an undercover police officer from the drugs squad who'd been commissioned to close this entire operation down.

'The journo doesn't take drugs!?' he hissed. 'Are you serious? How the fuck is he gonna write about this place if he doesn't take drugs?!'

'I don't know,' I shrugged. 'He seems to describe most things quite adequately.'

The tanned man in the fedora looked flummoxed.

'You mean he doesn't take *any* drugs,' he suddenly interjected. 'Not even coke?'

'No, nothing, ' I said. 'Not even coke.'

The man looked stunned—as if he'd found incontrovertible evidence for immortality—and walked over to Darren, where a heated discussion ensued. I noticed Darren glancing over at me several times. Eventually, the man returned and handed me a small bag.

'Here's some pills,' he said. 'If you can make the journo take one, all the better.'

And then off he disappeared, into the midday sun.

I'd still had no sleep, so I took one of the pills to see if that made any difference to my circumstances. It didn't. A man I recognised from the London club scene—or possibly the Gatwick Airport scene—wandered over and asked me if I was all right. I said I was fine, so he introduced me to his girlfriend.

'This is Dee,' he said. 'She came over here for a weekend a few years ago and loved it so much she never left.'

'How long have you lived here?' I asked.

'About seven years,' she said. 'Since 1990.'

For a moment I felt tempted to check my phone, but then I remembered: the year was definitely 2000.

Events got distinctly more odd after this moment; I suddenly began to develop warm and sincere feelings for everyone I was introduced to; the music, which had had only recently been fired up to crescendo levels, seemed to be beckoning me to go inside the building; and a beautiful woman with silver dreadlocks came over to talk to Saffron, Tim, and me. I was mesmerised, and when she left I whispered to Dee—or whoever seemed to be standing in her place, 'Who was that?'

'Oh, that's Mr C's wife,' she said. 'Did you like her?'

'Like her?' I said. 'She's got some kind of metal hair sown into her scalp. She's amazing.'

Saffron, Tim, and I decided it was time to enter the club, and I have to confess that I'd never seen anything like it; it was early Sunday afternoon, and people of all sizes and shapes were dancing on podiums or on each other's shoulders, looking like nothing else mattered. It was crazy, end-of-the-world stuff, and I loved it. What had I been missing my whole life?

Somehow, we lost track of Tim—or should that be time?—so I followed Saffron over to the DJ console—actually the size of a small city—where she threw her arms around Carl Cox, whom she knew well. Thereafter, over the next few hours, we ricocheted from one side of the club to the other, eventually emerging on a terrace to smoke cigarettes and calm down.

'I love Space,' I gushed, whilst gulping down a bottle of water.

'So do I,' said Saffron. 'But this isn't it.'

I must have looked confused, so Saffron explained to me that we had visited several clubs after leaving Space some time earlier in the afternoon. We were now in a club called DC10, situated so close to the airport that you could almost touch the undercarriage of every plane that came in to land. Each time anyone saw a plane on the horizon, the people around us would cheer raucously, waving their glasses in the air and toasting the new arrivals. My last recollection of the evening—or was it another morning?—is of Saffron being chased around the building by a bunch of dwarves who claimed to be in a band called Vertigo.

But Saffron and I endured, as did Tim, who surfaced just in time to write his two-page puff piece for the *Evening Standard*. He made twenty-four-hour clubbing sound much more organised—and indeed achievable—than it really was, but it set the tone nicely for the next stage of my PR tomfoolery: the opening party for the View Bar itself.

Of course, the View Bar was the only reason I'd taken on the project in the first place, since it was far easier to get people to write about a nascent private members' club venture than it was to write about another nightclub or another restaurant. I was nervous, nonetheless, but I needn't have worried: the View Bar may have had a capacity of around three hundred, but the sixty people I invited to the opening party all turned up, and, if you calculated my invite-to-acceptance success rate next to the rest of the hastily assembled committee's invite-to-acceptance success rate—if you don't already know, this is the mental calculation all event organisers and PRs make the minute they walk into an event they have organised—then you would have discovered that I was the overall winner. Which is the thought I was no doubt in possession of when I arrived at the View Bar looking suitably gorgeous.

I was wearing a blue agnès b. women's suit and sling-backs, and when I introduced myself to the numerous silver/glass/steel/mirrored elevator-door people, they seemed more animated than usual, and I sensed they were expecting riots. Whilst riots came there none, after I'd been ushered upstairs to the sixth floor, with more urgency than usual, I realised that anything could happen. A suitably convincing black transvestite eyed me cautiously/enviously as I arrived; the venue was rammed with the kind of attractive women I'd only ever seen in a 1970s Smirnoff advertisement; and I knew even more people than I would at a Suede show.

Of course, the truth of the matter is that my PR duties at the View Bar were more redundant than they had ever been at a Suede gig—at least at the latter I would memorise the set list and lyrics, so that I could help with journalist copy and then identify the right people to invite to the after-show. For an event as hifalutin as this, however, it was just a question of making sure everyone was getting legless. (Incidentally, I remember describing my job to my ninety-year-old grandmother as *dancing and giving people drinks whilst arranging for them to fly to Ibiza to have more drinks*, and she found this no more confusing than if I'd actually defined the authentic role of a PR—perhaps because the two descriptions were interchangeable.) And since the over-the-top catering would ensure that the free cocktails and canapés would be served until you were clinically deceased, then I needn't have turned up at all.

A lot of my friends—including Crispin and Rachael, Keith, Kieran, Saffron, Polly, Rachel, Grace—had turned out for *The Viewing*—all puns intended—but with a 1am curfew looming courtesy of Westminster Council's watertight anti-fun policy, it wasn't long before we'd all decided to decamp to a friend's house in Notting Hill to extend the festivities further.

Thirty of us made it to west London before Saffron whispered in my ear, 'Are the couple who live here swingers?'

'Yes, I think so,' I said. 'Why d'you ask?'

'Because someone said something, and I'm worried they might want to swing,' said Saffron.

'I don't think it works like that,' I said, without having any idea what either of us was talking about. 'I don't think they swing every day.'

'But still,' she said. 'They might want to swing tonight, and I don't feel comfortable here.'

And so Saffron and her friends left the premises.

Hours later, when the effects of several pills were peeking through, and the closest anyone got to swinging was whispering in each others ears, someone whispered the suggestion that we should all go and sit in a pub and pretend to order Sunday lunch. We rang our friend Tessa, who was at home with her Chihuahuas, and she arranged to meet us at the Westbourne.

Tessa Rock Chick was an infamous figure in the music world, having launched herself on the unsuspecting Brit rock fraternity by throwing parties for any visiting British pop star who happened to be passing through her home city of New York. The Gallagher Brothers had passed through her clutches/residence when they first visited the States in October 1994, and although I am assured nothing untoward occurred—who am I? The Queen Mother?— her reputation often preceded her.* Since moving to London, however, she'd stopped throwing parties and settled down quietly enough to be the proud owner of two cute Chihuahua puppies.

At the Westbourne, we ordered drinks, and I placed a Chihuahua on each of my shoulders. Tessa knew someone who would deliver coke to the area, so she handed me her phone, indicating that I should speak to the person on the other end.

'I'll be pulling up outside the Westbourne in about ten minutes,' said the voice. 'I'll be in a brown Rolls-Royce and wearing a hat'—I always find they wear hats—'but how will I recognise you?'

---

* I was lucky enough to see that first New York Oasis show at Wetlands on October 29 1994. In fact I had an argument with an American fan of the band who was standing next to me at the front of the gig, and who asked me at the end of the show whether I thought Liam had enjoyed performing.

'No,' I said, 'He doesn't get any pleasure playing for you guys.'

'What d'you mean?' he said, evidently hurt. 'He was tapping his foot all the way through the concert.'

'No he was not,' I insisted. 'He didn't tap his foot once, and he will never tap his feet whilst he is on American soil. Don't you get it? He hates America.'

The fan looked upset, but I didn't care—though quite why I'd take it upon myself to defend the reputation of a band I had never represented I don't know. Perhaps I was simply keen on promoting British nonchalance overseas.

'I'm wearing a blue agnès b. suit and sling-backs,' I suggested. 'Oh, and I've got a Chihuahua on each shoulder.'

Half an hour later, having completed an unsatisfactory transaction of sorts, I was sitting back down in the pub, pretending to eat my Sunday lunch.

The next day, in the office, I received a call from the owners of the View Bar, asking whether everything had gone swimmingly and my guests had enjoyed the event. I fudged over the fact that we had left early, declaring the evening *an unqualified success*. Perhaps this was almost entirely true, although it is difficult to tell since, several months later, the whole Home venture was shut down by Westminster Council after 'there was clear evidence of open drug-dealing at the club and the committee was duty-bound to revoke the public entertainment licence in the interests of public safety'. Well, not on my watch, I should point out, as I wasn't within a mile of the place, but it always struck me as odd that it should be closed down just as it became glaringly obvious that the venture was not going as well as expected. As to my own venture into dance music PR? Well, you could say I'd just about survived. I do have one regret, however: the super-club Home may have been spread over seven floors, but I never found out what happened on the first two. In my wildest dreams, it was a bridge club for gentle men and women.

This may have been Home's deepest, darkest secret.

CHAPTER 12

BOMBAY DREAMS

"It's a common assumption that heterosexual men are from towns like Wigan and Bolton and gay men are namby-pamby southerners. Naturally, having been born in Derby General Hospital—halfway between both destinations—I feel suitably qualified to comment on the subject."

I used to imagine that everyone who works at *GQ* magazine is gay while all the staff at *Attitude* are straight. This thought must have occurred to me when I rang up the editor of *Attitude* and asked if he would put Brett Anderson on the cover. We talked about Brett's gay credentials—he'd been quoted as saying he was 'a bisexual man who'd never had a homosexual experience' and regularly spanked his arse with a microphone—and, after some initial pleasantries, I got the impression that we were talking as two heterosexual men might do. When I enquired further, the editor even intimated that he was married to a real live woman.

'But how did you get the job?' I asked.

'I just came here for an interview and they gave it to me,' he said. 'They didn't ask about my living arrangements.'

I envisaged a reciprocal arrangement going on at *GQ*.

'*G*-bloody-*Q*,' a voice might proffer at the other end of the phone. 'Fashion, style, and culture for the discerning bloke. 'Ow may I direct your call?'

It's a common assumption that heterosexual men are from towns like Wigan and Bolton and gay men are namby-pamby southerners. Naturally, having been born in Derby General Hospital—*halfway* between both destinations—I feel suitably qualified to comment on the subject.

'I'd like to speak to your editor about Suede,' I say.

I can sense our intrepid anti-hero putting his hand over the receiver and all pretence of laddish-ness disappearing.

'Ooh, crikey,' I hear his muffled voice shout across the office floor. 'I've got that Suede PR on the phone. Get her if she doesn't want to speak to you!'

As I'd expected, the bluff northern phone technique was a front for a more covert operation.

Over at *Attitude*, the editor's thinly disguised telephonic mannerisms suggested I was really on to something.

'I've got that Phill fookin' Savidge on the fookin' phone,' he says, holding his hand over the receiver to ensure I am out of earshot—sounding not unlike a particularly riled Liam Gallagher. 'Fook me if he doesn't want us to put another screamer on the cover.'

There's a collective sigh—from you, dear reader—as we all acknowledge the futility of this artifice. And then? Silence. A moment of reflection.

Incidentally, I am acutely aware that gay men don't speak like this. However, for the purposes of this story, they do. I wonder, therefore, if seemingly contradictory scenarios aren't occurring all over London: *Tatler* is staffed by members of the Socialist Workers Party, and the *Morning Star* is manned by the landed gentry. And the *New Musical Express*? Are they employing people who don't know the first thing about music? I think we should be told.

In 2002, I sort of semi-represented Andrew Lloyd Webber for about a year, but I never got around to ringing *Attitude* about him. This is a shame, because Andrew has to be the no.1 non-mover in my Top 10 chart of Camp Men Who Are Not Actually Gay.

I'm no.2, but believe me there's a big gap keeping me off the top spot. All I know is that if you round off every dinner party at your house by passing around the score and script of *The Sound Of Music* and asking everyone if they would rather be Maria or any specific member of the Von Trapp family, plucked eyebrows are going to be raised.

He has a lovely house, mind you, and anyone who has his own elevator is all right by me. The first time I was called over for a breakfast meeting, I was struck by how much our taste in art coincided. On the walls of his living rooms and corridors he'd hung paintings by my favourite Pre-Raphaelite artists—John Everett Millais, Gabriel Dante Rossetti—and the extraordinary thing was that I had the very same paintings on the walls of my flat in Crouch End. What a coincidence, I thought, and then it struck me that there was a major difference: these were the originals! As he handed out croissants, Lloyd Webber barely noticed my lustful cravings for his bosom-bedecked facades, but I wonder if he thought, *Who is this person? In dungarees? And eyeliner? In my house!* I went so far as to ask Madeleine, his wife, where Andrew had hung my favourite painting, *The Death Of Chatterton* by Henry Wallis—a painting I'd only fallen in love with after reading Peter Ackroyd's novel *Chatterton*.

'Sshh,' she said. 'Andrew doesn't like to talk about it. It's the one painting he has always wanted to own, but it's hanging in the Tate.'

I was there to talk about A.R. Rahman—the Mozart of

Madras—multi-million, perhaps billion-selling Bollywood composer of Lloyd Webber's new musical, *Bombay Dreams*. I knew something of Rahman's work, having recently watched *Lagaan*, a hugely uplifting film about a village in India where the inhabitants are coerced into playing a three-day cricket match—against a team comprised of British officers—as a wager to avoid inordinately large taxes. I loved the film, and Rahman had composed a score that had proved immensely successful. Previous successes meant that Rahman was now one of the most famous men in the whole of India, and Andrew's people had asked me whether I was up to the task of ensuring that, by the time the musical opened, white men and women over here would be just as likely to recognise him as people in his home country. Of course, I soon realised there were about ten million naturalised Indian people over here that knew who he was already, but presumably, Andrew reckoned, they'd already have *Bombay Dreams* at the top of their must-see list.

One of Andrew's people (I'll stop saying this in a minute) pointed out that Rahman had sold about ten times as many records as Madonna and Kylie Minogue put together, so it was hardly surprising that I thought it pertinent to suggest a piece about Rahman's global significance in a British newspaper—and one featuring these two immediately recognisable Western pop icons. The natural choice was *News Of The World*, but due to an inherent distrust of anyone connected to The Man, no phone calls ever emanated from my ivory tour of Indie Goodness; instead I just waited for the call.* And, after a conversation between Lloyd Webber and *News Of The World* head honcho Stuart Kuttner at the House of Lords—I was there at the time but far too bashful to bring up the subject—I found myself in business.

A journalist called Rav Singh was chosen to accompany me on the trip to Chennai. At Heathrow, Rav and I laughed about the fact that his editor must have whooped with delight when he'd noticed a Singh amongst the ruins of his masthead. What better way to forge a handshake across two nations, we jested, and three cheers for Anglo–Indian relations! Of course, it turned out that it wasn't such a bad idea, since Rav's father was a Rahman obsessive and very keen on his son tracking down his hero in his natural habitat.

---

* I've always had a strange relationship with *The Sun* and *News Of The World*, mainly due to the fact that I am aware of what they can do to a person's life and career. Keith Allen once told me to 'keep your friends close and your enemies closer' when we were discussing tabloid newspapers and, as much as I know this as a borrowed sentiment, it also struck me as being rather glib, since the newspapers in question will discard their friends as quickly as their enemies.

Keith and I once went to Lahore—an Indian restaurant in Mile End—at midnight, and, as we walked in, we noticed that the entire staff of *The Sun* were dining out on a long table at the far end of the room. As one, they all seemed to rise up and shout 'Keeeeeeeeeeeth' as if he were their best and only friend in the entire world. Of course, I know that the only reason they acknowledged him at all was that his own star had risen further as the cheeky-chappy father of his rather more famous daughter, Lily, and, if they could keep up the pretence for a little while longer, they might be able to learn some tittle-tattle about her errant ways. (Well, that and the fact that they have no real friends anyway.) At the time, I wondered if the restaurant knew that the entire staff of Britain's biggest tabloid newspaper was sitting at its top table, whether, indeed, they might have been able to use the assembled throng to advertise its wares.

After a long day ruining lives, we at The Sun like to relax and dine in our favourite restaurant. Lahore … where evil people eat.

The Chennai trip was my first encounter with first-class travel, and I was hooked. Nothing was too much trouble, and champagne has always been my preferred beverage to accompany cornflakes. However, I was not used to everyone being so nice to me, particularly the air hostesses, who all seemed to be competing with each other for my hand in marriage. *Can I really be this desirable?* I thought, as they fetched my favourite newspaper and filled my glass for the third time. We hadn't yet taken off, and I was already feeling heady from my newfound fame. Were the air hostesses even now having an emergency meeting to discuss which one of them should be allowed to take me home for the evening? And who was I? A politician off to meet my overseas counterparts? Too young! An arms trader set to broker a deal on the subcontinent? Too nice!

The record producer Marius de Vries was also on the flight, as he'd been retained (amongst a wealth of other recording duties) to record a local orchestra at Rahman's house the day after we arrived. Dressed all in white—like a giant line of coke—he did a marvellous impression of someone who'd spent most of his life commuting first class to India; when we arrived at the hotel, he was the only one who knew what food to order, and how much energy we should be spending doing nothing at all. It turned out he'd picked the right clothes, too, since he didn't sweat the entire time we were out there.

Chennai seemed like an alien environment to me—rickshaws flanked our limousine, wheelchair-bound beggars blocked highway intersections—but Rahman's house was an oasis of tranquillity. Surrounded by trees in what passed for an opulent part of the city, I couldn't help noticing that several men were hanging around the entrance to his grounds when we arrived.

'Who are these people?' I asked our guide. 'Fans?'

No, he said, they're film producers desperate to catch Rahman's attention. If they can just shake his hand, pitch him a story, or pass him a script, then they're halfway to getting him to score their movie. With Rahman's name attached to a project, the film is guaranteed box office, and the soundtrack is sure to sell millions of copies.

The queue of men outside the gates continued inside the grounds, and I noticed two tents pitched near the front door. Apparently, not content with just *hanging around*, several producers had now decided to sleep next to the house so that they could confront Rahman in his pyjamas. We strode past several other smaller groups of men who all eyed us enviously as we began ascending the front steps of the house.

The entrance hall to Rahman's house was so dimly lit I had to squint to see what was around me. We were told to remove our shoes and don house slippers, and I could smell incense floating in from the hallway. Rahman came in to greet us, and I remember thinking it remarkable that someone so shy and unassuming should command such fuss from his countrymen. But it wasn't just his countrymen: Lloyd Webber and his entourage had flown halfway across the world to avail themselves of his talents.

Rahman's house was peculiarly big on the inside, like some

palatial Tardis with rooms shooting off in all directions. Rav and I were shown through to a large room containing a balcony, where we were invited to watch an orchestra performing something that would, eventually, one day, form part of the *Bombay Dreams* soundtrack. The song sounded how you might expect it to sound: essentially, Bollywood cannon fodder dressed up in stage tights and sequins. I hated musicals, but I thought the piece a marked improvement on anything else I'd heard in the genre.

After about half an hour, Rav and I were ushered out of the orchestra room and into a much smaller room. Three policemen greeted us and asked which one of us had the authority to sign some papers. I indicated that I had the authority, and there was an awkward silence before I realised that they were referring to the £30,000 of traveller's cheques I had brought over from the UK. Evidently, due to an inherent distrust of authority and the commissioning process, they needed me to sign the cheques before the orchestra would continue to play for more than an hour. I reached into my bag, pulled out the thirty individual cheques, and placed them on the table in front of me. I noticed that the orchestra had stopped playing.

It turned out that only one of the three men was a policeman. The other two were bank officials, whose presence was required to validate my signature. I signed the thirty separate documents whilst all three peered over my shoulder, checking for abnormalities in the undulations of my doctor's scrawl. All those years of practising my signature had really paid off.

I handed the final document over to one of the men who shuffled the papers for several seconds before indicating that he was satisfied with the arrangements. He then gestured to another man standing by the entrance to the room, and within moments the orchestra picked up where it had left off. The whole process took less than ten minutes. Rahman was nowhere to be seen.

Rav and I spent another hour or two at Rahman's house before deciding that we would soon die of boredom. We had also both begun to realise that the only reason we'd been invited in the first place is so that I could sign the traveller's cheques and the orchestra could continue to play. It seemed like a peculiar arrangement, but in India, cash (or the next best thing) is king, and no musician will work on the promise of being paid some day in the future. I had completed my work.

Well, not quite. Although, Rav now had some 'colour' for his piece (i.e. he'd checked out Rahman in his working environment), we still didn't have any pictures, and still less of an idea as to how to illustrate the level of fame A.R. Rahman had achieved in his homeland. We decided to go into the centre of Chennai to ask some of the locals what they thought about the legendary composer who lived in their midst.

Farewells were bade and taxis were called—yes, the idiosyncrasies of our distinctly individual roles in the operation meant that we took separate cabs—and soon we found ourselves on the sidewalk of one of the busiest streets in a suburb of the city. I was not used to stopping random people in the street and asking them for their opinion on a subject, but Rav seemed to take to it straight away. Perhaps it was his previous experience door-stepping pop stars who'd recently erred or ringing stricken PRs on Saturday mornings whilst they were still in their pyjamas, I don't know, but his brazen cheek surely has to be acknowledged. Locals whooped with delight when you mentioned Rahman's name, and suggestions that you'd shaken his hand less than half an hour ago brought about disbelieving glances followed by enquiries as to your sanity. But no, Rav ventured further, we'd just been to his house and had tea and crumpets. Cue, slaps on the back and—can you believe it?—requests for Rav's autograph.

But we still didn't have a story. I told Rav that we were wasting our time out on the street and we should try to find a location where we could take Rahman's picture the next day. I noticed some activity further down the street, where a collection of young men appeared to be crowding round the entrance to a shopping centre. Rav and I walked towards it, but as we got closer I realised it was really no more than a collection of badly organised grocery stores covered in a giant corrugated iron roof.

The grocery stores seemed to sell everything from pulses and lemons to shoes and records. One of them, in particular, had a huge selection of CDs and vinyl, so, more as a matter of instinct than interest, I started leafing through the selection. I was presented with the usual suspects—Dire Straits, Queen, Eagles—but other than this the store appeared to sell nothing but soundtracks to Indian movies, and most of them seemed to be recordings by

A.R. Rahman. I counted sixty different Rahman soundtracks and multiple copies of each.

Then I had an idea.

'Excuse me,' I said to the guy standing behind the counter. 'You've got an amazing selection of Rahman stuff here. Have you ever met him?'

The man stared blankly back at me.

'No,' he replied. 'I have never met him. In fact I've never seen him. He is very shy and he never goes out.'

'Really,' I say. 'That's very interesting, 'cos me and my friend here are over from England, and we've just been to his house to interview him. If you like,' I continued, 'we could get him to come in here to sign some of your records.'

'No,' the man repeated with more urgency. 'He will never come here. He is too shy, and he is afraid of being mobbed.'

'What if I can guarantee that he comes here to sign some records?' I suggested. 'Rav, have you got that letter from your editor, in case we had difficulty at the airport?' Rav reached into the inside pocket of his jacket and pulled out a piece of paper. I took it off him and handed it over to the storekeeper.

When the storekeeper read the letter, his face was transformed, as if he had just received a letter from the king. Which, when you think about it, he had. He threw the letter—rather disrespectfully, I thought—onto the rack of CDs in front of him and reached into a drawer, pulling out a gun. Then, with much excitement, he pointed the gun up into the air and pulled the trigger, twice firing off into the corrugated iron roof above the shop. Instantly, two pieces of ceiling tile dislodged themselves before he fired the gun twice again. Eventually, he put the gun down and picked up a loudhailer lying on the counter.

'A.R. RAHMAN WILL BE HERE TO-MORR-OW,' he yelled into the loudhailer. 'A.R. RAHMAN WILL BE HERE TO-MORR-OW TO SIGN RECORDS. COME TO THE STORE AT THIS TIME TO-MORR-OW, AND I CAN GUARANTEE THAT A.R. RAHMAN WILL BE HERE TO SIGN RECORDS.'

The effect of his words was immediate. Several men I'd hardly been aware of before suddenly started to shake visibly, and one or two wailed uncontrollably as if in the midst of a transcendental experience. Their words were unintelligible to me, but the men seemed inconsolable with both happiness and madness in equal measure. One or two produced handguns, firing into the air and causing more corrugated iron to splinter and debris to fall around us. There was pandemonium, but in amongst it I heard Rahman's name being chanted with greater and greater urgency.

I was concerned I had caused a scene of such significant religious ferocity that my name would be lauded in local circles for several generations to come, so I suggested to Rav that we should leave the scene immediately. Of course, both of us now realised that we had to organise a photograph of the following day's proceedings as a matter of urgency. Rav made a phone call—who was I gonna call?—and within five minutes he received a call back from a News International photographer who lived in Chennai and had been commissioned from London to photograph the proceedings.

I also got a call during this episode, and it was from Rahman's people—almost certainly entirely distinct from Lloyd Webber's people, who'd presumably now retired to a local palace more in keeping with their circumstances—who requested that Rav and I should make ourselves presentable to attend a dinner at a restaurant that evening hosted by Rahman. *So he does go out*, I thought. And tonight will be the only chance to tell him what I've got in mind for tomorrow night.

The dinner was in the most delightful restaurant about ten minutes from our hotel, and when we arrived several local dignitaries were waiting in reception for Rahman's arrival. Or should that mean for Rav and I to arrive? It's difficult to be certain, because when we turned up we were afforded the kind of attention usually reserved for the very rich and famous. Yes, you've guessed it: word had got out that we were the British pair that had made Rahman come out of his shell.

It is difficult to explain how famous Rahman is in his home country, as the reference points don't quite seem to equate to the ones we are used to. It's not just that his celebrity is somehow up there with the combined fame of Michael Jackson, Elvis Presley, John Lennon, and David Bowie put together, it's just that all of these artists inspired as much indifference as love throughout their homelands; in India, there are no dissenting voices with regard to Rahman—he is a spiritual, royal, and secular presence rolled into one.

Somehow, after much deliberation and elbowing my way into Rahman's peripheral vision, I managed to ask him if he could make himself available for the public appearance I had organised for the following day. When I told him the nature of the arrangements, his face fell, as if he had just received news that one of his closest relatives had passed away suddenly. But he knew he had to do something to make sure that our trip wasn't wasted. I wondered if his role as part of the *Bombay Dreams* project depended on his compliance with Western publicity demands.

Whatever his motives, Rahman agreed to turn up at the supermarket the following day, and when Rav and I arrived— around an hour before his scheduled appearance—I guessed there were at least a thousand people crowded around the entrance. We fought our way through to the mall inside, spoke to the storekeeper, and introduced ourselves to the photographer, who seemed as bemused as anyone. I told the photographer he should find a comparatively calm vantage point on the first floor of the building, so that he could look down on the chaos beneath.

Rahman arrived sitting on an ornate chair—by which I mean to say, he got as close as he could to the entrance, and then his minders produced the chair, he sat in it, and four of them carried him above the heads of the crowd into the building. Inside, there was uproar, more shots were fired, and Rahman's name was being chanted over and over again. Rahman dismounted from his chair and began signing shirts, CDs, and any piece of paper thrust under his nose. The atmosphere was charged with tension, but

LUNCH WITH THE WILD FRONTIERS

his disciples so gentle and respectful, that at no point did I think the situation menacing. I glanced up at the photographer, who was snapping away furiously. My last image was of the storekeeper grasping hundreds of CDS and ushering Rahman to come and join him sitting behind the counter.

Three weeks later, the *News Of The World* ran a centre-page spread featuring images of Madonna and Kylie Minogue at its borders and a huge, extraordinary shot of Rahman being carried above the crowds at the supermarket in Chennai. Question: who sells more records than Kylie Minogue and Madonna put together? Answer: he's sitting in the chair. Rahman had made his first breakthrough in the UK.

Except we know different, don't we? Because every time I walked down the street with Rahman in Kensington or Soho or Shoreditch or Peckham (OK, I made the last one up, there's no such place), hundreds of Asian people knew exactly who Rahman was, and it seemed to me I was wasting my time making him famous for the white community. Some weeks after the Chennai trip, I had to introduce Rahman to Prince Charles—not an easy thing to do when you don't know Prince Charles in the first place, and he is in a bad mood because his dog has just died—at the Asian Business Awards, and again there was no problem getting Rahman recognised. And when *Bombay Dreams* was first performed at the Apollo Victoria Theatre on June 19 2002, almost everyone seemed to know exactly who Rahman was. Apart from Christopher Biggins, that is, who made sure he knew everyone else.

CHAPTER 13

ENDING UP
IN THE
HOSPITAL

"If Paul accidentally dropped $10,000 down the back of the sofa, it would not be worth the minute or so it would take to find it, since he would already have earned that money in interest in the time it took to respond to its loss."

There's a scene in *Blackadder Goes Forth* (episode 2, 'Corporal Punishment') where Captain Blackadder gets court-martialled and then sentenced to death by firing squad. Lieutenant George, his incompetent sidekick, suddenly realises he can halt Blackadder's execution by writing to his Mad Uncle Rupert, who is Minister Of War with 'power over life and death, and who'll be able pull strings and scratch backs and fiddle with knobs'. The realisation catapults George and his even more incompetent companion in arms, Baldrick, into such a state of euphoric unrest that they begin to celebrate 'with a toss of old Morehen's Shredded Sporum', which George's mother had just sent over from England. Needless to say, the relentless toasting of their cleverness, and Blackadder's inevitable good fortune, forces them to neglect to send any telegram whatsoever, and when they wake up the following morning, they are filled with remorse at having sent Blackadder to his death. Of course, Blackadder survives George's ineptitude— doesn't he always?—strolling into the trenches the next day to reveal that Uncle Rupert had actually sent a second telegram to George (which Blackadder had intercepted) and been surprised George hadn't contacted him in the first place.

I only mention this because a similar thing happened to me when I bumped into Dave Stewart in Covent Garden at the turn of the century. I'd obviously known Dave for many years, ever since I'd been charged with representing Curve back in 1990, but the Dave I'd encountered more recently seemed to have a chaotic lifestyle involving houses in France, Surrey, and central

London. His house in Surrey I thought grand but unloved—it had a skateboard court for his two boys, which he told me they'd used only once—but his Seven Dials residence in Covent Garden was something else altogether; the entire apartment was furnished with fibre-optic carpets, and all windows could be blacked out or brightened up with a mere touch of a button. One night after I ended up there, Dave pressed another button and a bed rose from the floor. There was nothing sexual implied or indeed intended, and I got the same feeling I always got from being around Dave— he was as excited as I was by seeing what *they* would come up with next. Later that same evening, I retired to the tiniest space in the apartment, and sat/slept/swung in a hanging basket acquired for just such purposes. It was here that I discovered Dave's Andy Warhol wig. I'm not going to say that it was the same wig that Andy Warhol used to wear for public appearances, but I think it might have been the very same wig that Andy Warhol wore for public appearances.

Of course, this brings us back to how we got here in the first place: Dave and I somehow lost touch, and when we bumped into each other in Covent Garden in the year 2000, we were both genuinely pleased to see each other. The likely story was that Dave had been trying to get hold of me for months, and when he dragged me down some side street to show me the latest project he was working on, I thought my ship had come in.

I wasn't even sure it was his office. Dave was dressed in a white suit, and the office I now found myself in was so white you could

243

feel yourself blushing at your lack of cleanliness. He appeared to know everyone in the building, but when he showed me into an even whiter office, I thought I was going blind. He opened a laptop, and an enormous image appeared on the wall. The image was of an island shaped like a palm tree. Apparently, I was to be charged with the task of making this island famous.

Of course, I now realise that Dubai's Palm Island project needed me to publicise its existence as much as I needed to get out of this white emporium as quickly as possible, but I was excited nonetheless. Particularly when Dave mentioned the real reason he'd brought me into the building: the Hospital.

The Hospital, I learned, had been Dave's vision for many, many years: a private members' club housing some of the youngest, finest, most creative minds on the planet. Forget Palm Island; here lay *The Future Of All Creativity*. Dave had always been obsessed with Andy Warhol and the Factory—indeed, he'd once asked me whether I wanted to be Candy Darling in a photograph he wanted to recreate for the *Sunday Times Magazine*; I remembered the original photograph, and Candy being naked, and decided not to do it—and this was his chance to realise his dream.

Dave's modern-day Factory would be a place where likeminded individuals—those from the creative industries—would be able to mingle together and discuss their latest artistic endeavours. In addition, the club's nominated, vetted members would be able to use several 'bat phones' resident on site; the moment anyone had the slightest piece of inspiration for a movie or art project, they could pick up one of these phones, pitch their project, and apply for funding. Once they'd replaced the receiver, they'd only have to wait a few minutes before receiving a reply. Indeed, there were suggestions that when the phone rang it would throb bright red, just like the one in the *Batman* TV series.

Dave explained that the Hospital would also feature an *Artist In Residence* programme where *Very Important Artists* would live and work on the top floor of the building for one month at a time. The Artist In Residence would curate the building—theme it, if you will—with some of the projects they had been involved in over the years, while also showcasing some of their favourite artists' works. These latter works might be under-promoted or just particularly relevant to the Artist In Residence's career, but it was all to be part of a nurturing environment encouraged by the Hospital. And the AIR programme in general appeared to be a permanent, living embodiment of Meltdown, the annual festival for music, art, performance, and film held on the South Bank. Rumours were that Dennis Hopper had already agreed to be the first Artist In Residence. And Martin Scorsese had agreed to be second.

The Hospital Project was to be funded by Microsoft's Paul Allen, one of Dave's closest friends and one of the richest men in the world. Indeed, I already knew Paul to be worth around $20 billion, and I had heard an interesting anecdote about his fortune: if Paul accidentally dropped $10,000 down the back of the sofa, it would not be worth the minute or so it would take to find it, since he would have already earned that money in interest in the time it took to respond to its loss. I imagined Paul clutching envelopes containing $10,000 increments and discarding them nonchalantly towards the back of any sofas he should come across.

It's possible that Dave and Paul had actually first conceived the idea of the Hospital whilst on an hallucinogenic trip at Dave's flat in Seven Dials; when discussing the possibility of creating a modern day Factory, they had both looked out the window at the same time, noticed the old, disused building—actually an old VD clinic—at the end of the road, and realised it would make the perfect plot for their plans. Perhaps Paul was wearing Dave's Andy Warhol wig at the time, I don't know, but I do know that, with the casual indifference that only the mega-rich can afford, Paul immediately agreed to buy it.

Whilst Dave was telling me all this, my heart was pounding, as I realised I was being afforded the gig of a lifetime. My thoughts were already drifting to a place where hundreds of Paul's envelopes were falling down the back of my sofa when I realised that Dave was still speaking to me.

'Can you come to my office in Covent Garden tomorrow morning at 8am?' he suggested. 'I'll show you some of the plans for the Hospital, and we can talk about how we can go about publicising it. I also want to talk to you about putting the committee together and recruiting founder members.'

'Of course,' I said, and we shook hands on the deal. The white suit remained un-crumpled.

I was so excited by the prospect of working with Dave and Paul—and subsequently becoming one of the richest people in the world—that I immediately rang my coke dealer and ordered five grams of coke. I then rang my flatmates/lodgers, Pat and Jo Skinny, to tell them my good news, and that they should prepare themselves for a night of hedonism back at the converted church we called home.* Two hours later, after the coke arrived and we had sampled several lines, we were dancing round the living room listening to Faithless, Underworld, and a whole cupboard full of Fluke records I'd reserved for occasions such as this. Talk quickly turned to my new role as the creative force behind the most ambitious artistic project in London, and we all agreed that the champagne needed to be opened and drunk as quickly as possible. Before too long we'd all taken an E, and the last thing I remember is Jo sitting on a wine glass and her bum having bits of glass sticking out of it.

We'd ordered so much coke that there was never any danger of running out, and by the time it got to six o'clock in the morning I knew I wasn't going to make the meeting with Dave. I was a mess, still wearing the same clothes I'd been wearing when we'd met the day before, and the thought of him turning up in a pristine white suit—presumably a different white suit, extracted from a

---

* Pat and Jo were—they still are!—a boyfriend-and-girlfriend stylist couple who I'd become close friends with, and when their London pied-à-terre fell through, I offered to put them up. They were extremely influential in the look of many Britpop artists of the era, and uncommonly good-looking enough to feature in several Britpop videos, including Pulp's 'Disco 2000'.

symmetrical selection of perfectly aligned white suits hanging in his perfectly situated white wardrobe—made me feel slightly nauseous. My less debauched version of old Morehen's Shredded Sporum had finally done for me, and I was never going to own my own supersonic yacht.

The last two hours before the meeting were spent pacing the room, snorting more coke, smoking evermore furiously, and calling a cab. The cab never materialised, and it's quite possible that I never called it in the first place. However, its non-arrival did spur me into a new course of action: I would call Dave's office, speak to his PA, and suggest that I had been badly let down by the London black cab taxi service. Hadn't we all been let down at some point? And didn't the fact that I was now ringing her office at 8am, to suggest there was a problem with my cab, indicate that I was the kind of person that always got up early, hailed cabs, and attended meetings just like the one that Dave and I had arranged?

I was pretty sure that Dave's PA believed every word I was saying, but I could hear her conversing with Dave in the background, and he didn't seem all that pleased. Eventually, she returned to the phone and informed me that Dave had made a special effort to come into town early that morning, and yes, I'd guessed it, he wasn't all that pleased. However, if I agreed to meet him at his office at the same time the following morning, then all would be forgiven, and we could pick up from where we'd left off. I was off the hook; crisis averted.

Pat, Jo, and I carried on partying for the next few hours before retiring, each of us in turn no doubt figuring that if we were ever going to resume normal service then normal activities like sleep needed to be resumed as soon as possible. When we resurfaced during the mid-afternoon lull of nothingness, we made the momentous decision to order Chinese food for later that evening. Such are the vagaries of a freelance life. No wonder our yachts were circling the church with little chance of disembarkation.

I met Dave at the agreed time the following morning, and we discussed how I was to turn the Hospital into the most talked-about building in the capital. I suggested articles in the *Financial Times* and *Vogue* magazine, and it wasn't long before we were shaking hands again and I was off making phone calls. Two weeks later, I showed *Vogue* some detailed plans of the building, told them all about the bat phone and the Artist In Residence programme, and they agreed to photograph Dave in his Covent Garden apartment. The results became a six-page feature on the Hospital—or, if you like, a puff piece about a building that had yet to be built.

Astonishingly, the notoriously shy Paul Allen agreed to be photographed alongside Dave for the cover of the *FT* magazine. The shoot was due to take place amongst the foundations of the Hospital itself, but when I arrived there was no sign of Paul or Dave. Instead, I was confronted by two FBI officers who'd been dispatched to check out the building prior to Paul's arrival. No doubt this was a service offered to all US billionaires when they made public appearances, so I pointed the two agents in the direction of the foreman, and then watched whilst they chatted then fingered their hard hats apprehensively. Half an hour later, Paul and Dave were photographed looking similarly confused and wearing the very same hard hats.

After the initial flurry of press interest, I set about sourcing potential Hospital committee and founder members. This proved simple enough, since I'd been charged with a similar task when I was asked to be on the original committee of Soho House some years before. However, the proposition for membership of the Hospital—or *The Quest For The Ideal Member (Part II)*—appeared elusive. The Soho House concept had been quite straightforward—would any young person in the creative industries like to get together in a private, social environment and, er, hang out? That's it! In contrast, the Hospital seemed to have this rather nebulous notion that there was something else they needed to offer; potential members needed to announce their credentials as a battle cry and embrace mentoring as a concept; every time the newly formed committee got together, fierce debates raged within, and a consensus was never achieved. Inevitably, every meeting—always accompanied by the finest canapés and finest drinks supplied by the finest catering companies, keen to be retained once the Hospital opened its doors—dissolved into confused laughter and indecision.

It seemed like the most natural of natural developments when the higher echelons of the organisation, with nothing better to do and Paul Allen's money to spend, commissioned a marketing group to help them to decide what to actually *name* the Hospital.

For me, this seemed absolutely absurd: what could be better than *The Hospital*? Indeed, what more evocative sentence could there be than *I had such a good time on Friday night that I ended up in the Hospital?* However, the brave men and women in marketing-land were used to tackling problems like this standing on their heads, and I couldn't be sure that they hadn't come up with most of their hare-brained suggestions whilst actually doing so. I'm certain that several tens of thousands of pounds were spent coming up with the suggestion *Tarantula*—since the Hospital had so many legs in its armour (they've already got me mixing my metaphors), only a moniker of such complexity would suit the organisation's multifaceted nature—but when we were asked to bring something worth less than a pound to the next marketing think-in, I realised the game was up: the idea had been to bring in an inanimate object that would sum up the Hospital's philosophy; naturally, some bright spark brought in a Percy Pig and immediately struggled to come up with anything intelligible to say about it. Hardly surprising, since they'd obviously bought it in the local shop on the way to the meeting.

Of course, there were many other marketing initiatives to be pursued: on May 18 2005, I was asked to organise a photograph by Richard Young of George Lucas and Paul Allen on Paul's boat, *Octopus*, which, at the time, was moored just outside Cannes. *Octopus*, at 414 feet in length, was the biggest privately owned ocean liner in the world, and featured a crew of sixty, plus seven boats, two helicopters, a recording studio, a *Yellow Submarine*, and an on-deck open-air concert venue about as big as Brixton Academy. The boat cost £12 million a year to run and £500,000 to fill up with fuel, but I was far more interested in Dave's living quarters, which were a cross between the *Starship Enterprise* and a Paul Schrager hotel. Dave was as astonished as I was that such a place existed, but at least he had the good fortune to have more reason to be there than I did. As soon as he took me to his cabin, he called his wife, Anoushka, on the house phone, and her face appeared on the big screen in front of us. She was in Los Angeles, and I don't know whether this was an early version of Skype or some kind of special, nascent Paul Allen–created technology, but all three of us seemed to laugh at the insanity of it all. Things were about to get stranger.

Back on deck, I spoke to the right people and grabbed Paul's attention so that I could double check what time George Lucas was due on board. Paul seemed disinterested, though I suspected this to be a regular ploy employed by the rich and/or famous: *Oh, there's a photo call? I didn't realise! Who's it with again? Oh, George! Well. If someone wants me to do it then I suppose I should do it!* I was intrigued, however, by the very much younger version of Paul (complete with glasses and nerd suit) hovering in Paul's vicinity throughout the evening. He carried a tiny laptop and typed furiously whilst we conversed. I learned later that he was Paul's *Four-Minute Man*, a man who inhabited a world four minutes into the future: Paul's plans could change at any moment, and if he suddenly decided, mid-conversation, that he needed to be in

New York, Beirut, or Athens on the following day, *Four-Minute Man* needed to be well prepared; Paul might dive into one of the rooms on *Octopus*, and there he would find a laptop and a bottle of water prepared in advance. And when he awoke at some unspecified time and in some unspecified location during the next morning, and his favourite pants and socks were already packed into his favourite suitcase, then *Four-Minute Man* had done his job.

Later that evening, when George Lucas arrived by helicopter and finally jumped out, I noticed his hair didn't actually move, even though the blades of the helicopter were revolving so fiercely that the rest of us were pegged back against some decking. Somehow, without being flattened, Paul and George shook hands, and Richard and I ushered the pair of them over to the far side of the boat so that he could take the picture. Afterwards, Paul and George shook hands again, and arrangements were made for the evening ahead. The next time I saw Paul, he was on the massive stage of the *Octopus*—next to the two helicopter pads—performing with Dave and the rest of his rock band. He was actually a pretty good guitarist, and, what with the champagne and the exalted company I now found myself in, and my first stolen look at the *Yellow Submarine* in the hold, I made the decision to quite like him.

The Hospital was not all plain sailing. (You see what I did there?) Subsequently, Paul found he had to pay millions of pounds towards 'affordable housing' for the residents who lived in close proximity to the area immediately surrounding the Hospital. His was to placate the local council as much as the local populace. There were intensive and intrusive building works, to be sure, but I did get the feeling that some of the local inhabitants smelt small fortunes and behaved accordingly. *Oh, the noise is playing terrible havoc with my nerves, I live a quarter of a mile away* does not strike me as the best line of defence when asked to provide reasons for compensation—but it worked. Subsequently, several other self-interested and self-fulfilling rumours were passed around, and it wasn't long before the building was being referred to as *Dave's Disco*. Meanwhile, Hospital marketing had gone into overdrive: we may have got away with *Tarantula*, but how about *The Hub*? And *Fulcrum*? You couldn't make it up.

Whilst all this was going on, Dave had asked me whether I'd be able to organise some publicity around his recording of the *Alfie* soundtrack—a score he'd recently recorded with Mick Jagger to accompany the remake of the movie, starring Jude Law and Sienna Miller. Dave was rightly worried that he'd be forgotten amongst the attendant furore surrounding Jagger's involvement, and that employing a PR to accompany him on the red carpet for the UK premiere would mitigate these issues somewhat. He couldn't have been more wrong.

On the day of the premiere, most of the talk seemed to revolve around whether Law and Miller, who were presumed to be having an affair, would arrive separately or together, or would even be willing to be photographed together, given the nature of their relationship. Dave and I were a sideshow at best, and when I arrived with Dave in Leicester Square, I was acutely conscious that I was out of my depth. There were hundreds of reporters from all over the world, and apart from some of the UK-based paparazzi and a couple of BBC arts reporters, I barely knew any of them. Dave seemed happy enough to wander up and down the banks of reporters, speaking to whoever would have him, but I knew this was never going to be good enough. And when Jagger's PR, Bernard Doherty, arrived, I had a deep sense of foreboding.

Bernard and I briefly said hello, but within minutes he was on his phone, speaking to Jagger.

'Mick,' he'd say. 'Where are you? Ten minutes away? Great. Just drive around for a bit.' Then he'd put the phone down again and talk to a reporter for a few seconds. Then the phone would ring again. 'Hi Mick,' he'd say. 'Where are you? Eight minutes away? That's great. Just drive around for a bit. No, everyone's here. They're all waiting for you. How's L'Wren? Great. See you in a bit.' Then Bernard would speak to more reporters until the phone rang again. This whole process went on for the ten minutes that it took Mick Jagger to drive painfully slowly from somewhere in the Leicester Square area to Leicester Square itself.

When Jagger arrived in Leicester Square, he seemed slightly nervous, if somewhat possessed of the usual rhetoric associated with those pretending they don't know what all the fuss is about. *Me? All this for me? Surely not!* He didn't seem particularly interested in any of the reporters surrounding him, just getting to

Bernard as quickly as possible. And when Bernard grabbed hold of him, and they both started to walk down the red carpet, they were professionalism personified. They made a lovely couple.

'Bernard!' a reporter would shout. And then another. 'Bernard!' 'Bernard! Sky News, can we have a word?' said another. 'BBC News,' said someone else. 'Bernard, Fox News,' said another. It was extraordinary. No one shouted Jagger's name throughout the entire time we were on the red carpet; they all just wanted to grab Bernard's attention, so that he'd deliver his prize. And that was my problem: none of these reporters knew my name, so they just ended up shouting for Dave. I'm sure Dave watched the whole process unravel and realised that we were never going to stop this juggernaut. And I resolved to get out of the publicity business as quickly as possible.

* * *

A year later, Dave rang me up and said that he wanted me to show Lou Reed around the Hospital. Lou and Dave were great friends, and during a recent conversation Dave had mentioned to Lou that he'd founded a club called the Hospital that was intended as a modern-day version of the Factory. Seeing as Lou had been such an intimate part of the original Factory, would he like to take a look around and let him know what he thought? And, seeing as I owned pretty much every Velvet Underground recording in existence, I happily agreed.

On the day of Lou's visit, I decided to wear a suit. I don't know why I did this, but I wanted to look smart. It was a women's suit, of course, and I hoped that the quirkiness of this choice might impress on Lou my credentials for the role of tour guide; finally I could be the Hospital's Candy Darling.

When he arrived in reception, Lou looked older and far frailer than I'd imagined, but he was also very sweet, which was somewhat surprising, as I'd heard he could be a cantankerous old sod. We shook hands and then took the elevator to the second floor—the main hive of activity.

'What kind of place is this?' asked Lou, in the lowest voice I had ever heard.

'Oh you know,' I said. 'It's a creative environment for young people in the creative industries—film, music, TV, art—so they can collaborate together and produce exciting projects. It's kind of based on the Factory.'

When Lou and I alighted on the second floor, we passed through to the club space, where several men in casual suits worked away on their laptops. None of them looked up when we walked in, and it is quite possible that if any of them had, none of them would have recognised Lou Reed, nor even owned a single Velvet Underground record. Lou seemed unimpressed, though it was difficult to be certain, since, in real life—by which I mean, on television—he always seemed unimpressed.

We went to several other spaces to look at more men and several women wearing suits and staring at laptop screens before Lou got a call saying that his wife, Laurie, was downstairs. We descended in the elevator in silence. In the lobby, Laurie Anderson and Lou greeted each other with a friendly kiss and held hands whilst we looked around the ground floor of the building. They seemed to be very much in love.

The following day, I rang Dave and said that I'd very much enjoyed showing Lou round the Hospital, as he was one of my heroes.

'Did he enjoy the experience?' I asked. 'What did he say about the Hospital?'

'He said it's not like the Factory,' said Dave.

A NEW MORNING

"I am the lead singer of Suede, Pulp, Elastica, Kula Shaker, and Fat Les; I used to spank my arse with a microphone, my inter-song banter is as good as the songs themselves, I used to look like a boy but my ex-boyfriends are more famous than I am, I am handsome, pretentious, and privileged—but I shall never see me in concert."

That was not the end. This is.

When I met my First And Only Wife, we decided to sell the maisonette I'd lived in for the last five years so that we could move to a house and start our new life together. I asked an estate agent to come to our flat for a valuation. When he arrived, the sun was streaming down and he was in shirtsleeves, a jacket casually draped over one shoulder; he looked like Tony Blair ready to board his election battle bus. He bounded around the house with gay abandon, before it became patently obvious that he had to say something.

'I hope you don't mind me asking,' he said, gesturing at the collection of gold discs along the walls of my home—items I had only removed from the cellar for his benefit. 'Are you still performing?'

I thought about saying, *Yes, that's right. I am the lead singer of Suede, Pulp, Elastica, Kula Shaker, and Fat Les; I used to spank my arse with a microphone, my inter-song banter is as good as the songs themselves, I used to look like a boy but my ex-boyfriends are more famous than I am, I am handsome, pretentious, and privileged—but I shall never see me in concert—and I am the leader of an event-led, anarcho-pop art collective whose output has seen better days. I am all these things and more.*

Instead, I said, 'Yes, but not as often as I'd like to.'

* * *

On July 16 2002, Suede were due to launch their fifth and possibly final album, *A New Morning*, with a 'secret' show at

Camden's Electric Ballroom. The show was superb, and I thought songs like 'Obsessions' and 'Lost In TV' were as good as anything I had ever heard by the band. I was excited to be working on a new campaign, imagining all the fun I would have, pitting one magazine against another.

After the show, I hung around in the foyer, soaking in the atmosphere with the rest of the diehard fans who'd been waiting for a new Suede record for as long as I had.

'Excuse me,' said a voice from behind me. I turned around and saw that the voice belonged to a boy barely out of his teens. 'I wonder if you can help me?'

'Sure,' I said. 'What's the problem?'

The boy tapped his foot before producing a notebook from the satchel he was carrying over his shoulder.

'Do you mind if I ask you a few questions?' he asked tentatively. 'I mean about the gig.'

'No,' I said, 'fire away.'

The boy looked down at his pad.

'What did you think of the gig?' he said.

'Amazing,' I replied. 'One of the best gigs I've ever seen.'

The boy wrote something down on the pad.

'What about the new songs?' he said. 'Do you like them?'

'Yes,' I replied. 'Excellent stuff. They're on top form.'

The boy scribbled something else down.

'What about your friends?' he continued. 'Did they like the new songs?'

'I think so,' I said. 'But I haven't had a chance to talk to anyone since the gig finished.'

By now, I had started to feel concerned, since the boy seemed to be writing down everything I told him.

'Look, I said. 'I'm not being funny, but I'm probably not the best person to be answering questions about Suede, since I've seen them live about a hundred times, and I've been their publicist ever since their first single. Why are you asking me all these questions?'

The boy looked at me for a moment, as if deciding on his next course of action.

Eventually, he said, 'I work for a marketing agency, and we've been employed by the *New Musical Express* to find out what young people think of the new Suede record. The results will determine whether they decide to give the band any coverage or not.'

For the first time in my life, I didn't know what to say, so I smiled at the boy and walked away.

When *A New Morning* was released on September 30, a team of marketing executives ensured that it wasn't particularly well received. It wasn't particularly dismissed out of hand, either; I can only assume that the lack of consensus within this executive caucus was a determining factor.

The *NME* gave the record seven out of ten. They didn't put Suede on the cover.

In my favourite film, *Withnail & I*, Withnail's drug-peddling

chum, Danny, laments the end of *the greatest decade*—the 60s—
thus: 'They're selling hippie wigs in Woolworths, man.'

Decades on, *they* don't sell anything unless you've already
bought it first. Woolworths has since ceased trading, and the
NME only exists as an online source for the uninitiated.

Perhaps that's where market research gets you in the end.

Time stands still, but I continue to operate as if it is moving.

CAST OF CHARACTERS

Damon Albarn Lead singer of British rock band Blur; co-founder of virtual band Gorillaz.

Keith Allen British actor, comedian, and musician. Co-writer of New Order's only UK no.1 single, 'World In Motion'. Formed Fat Les and co-penned the 1998 World Cup anthem 'Vindaloo'.

Paul Allen Microsoft co-founder and billionaire. Founder (along with Dave Stewart) of the Hospital Club in Covent Garden (d. October 15 2018).

Brett Anderson Lead vocalist of Suede, solo artist, and author of *Black Coal Mornings*.

Richard Ashcroft British solo artist and songwriter and lead singer of The Verve.

David Bailey British fashion and portrait photographer who was the inspiration for the London fashion photographer featured in Michelangelo Antonioni's *Blow Up*.

Lynn Barber British journalist (*Observer, Sunday Times*) famed for her shrewd interview technique.

Michael Barrymore	British TV presenter of game shows who was considered one of the most popular UK performers in the 1990s.
Mel Bell	Founder of Mel Bell Publicity in the 1980s.
John Best	Manager of The Verve, founder of Best In Press, and co-founder of Savage & Best. Best now manages Icelandic avant-rock superstars Sigur Ros.
Polly Birkbeck	Ex Food Records employee and Savage & Best PR 1993–99.
David Bowie	British singer, songwriter, and actor (d. January 10 2016).
William Burroughs	American writer and visual artist and primary figure of the Beat Generation (d. August 2 1997).
Bernard Butler	British musician, songwriter, and record producer. One of Britain's most influential guitarists, he was lead guitarist with Suede for their first two albums, *Suede* and *Dog Man Star*.
Mary Byker	Singer, producer, and DJ known for his work as lead singer with Gaye Bykers On Acid.
Jonathan Carricker	Former bassist for UK-based band Kill Devil Hills.

Jarvis Cocker	British musician, TV and radio presenter, and lead singer of Pulp.
Andrew Collins	British writer and broadcaster who wrote for the *NME* and *Select*; editor of *Q* between 1995 and 1997.
Tim Cooper	*Sunday Times* and London *Evening Standard* journalist.
Sian Davies	Head Of Press at Virgin Records in the 1980s and 1990s.
Bernard Doherty	Rolling Stones publicist; CEO and co-founder of LD Communications.
José Férez	Art curator and author, and mentor to William Burroughs.
Justine Frischmann	A founder member of Suede, Frischmann is best known as the lead singer of Britpop stars Elastica. She now pursues a successful career as a painter.
Peter Gabriel	British singer, songwriter, record producer, and founder/frontman of progressive-rock band Genesis, whom he left in 1975 to pursue a solo career. Owner of Real World Studios and Real World Records.
Charlotte Gainsbourg	French actress and singer; daughter of English actress Jane Birkin and songwriter Serge Gainsbourg.

Saul Galpern	Nude Records label boss who signed both Suede and Ultrasound.
Luke Haines	A British musician, songwriter, and author, Haines has recorded music as The Auteurs, Baader Meinhof, and Black Box Recorder.
John Harris	British journalist, writer, and critic; author of *Britpop, Blair, And The Demise Of English Rock*.
Rachel Hendry	Savage & Best PR from 1994 to 1999.
Damien Hirst	British artist, entrepreneur, and art collector who won the Turner Prize in 1995 and has dominated the UK art scene ever since. Nominally part of the Fat Les collective that spawned 'Vindaloo' and 'Jerusalem' at the turn of the century.
Darren Hughes	Club promoter (Home, Space) and former co-owner of Liverpool's Cream club.
Crispin Hunt	Ex-vocalist for Sheffield band Longpigs, Hunt has since written for a huge variety of artists, including Ellie Goulding, Florence & The Machine, and Jake Bugg.
Mick Jagger	Lead singer and founder member of The Rolling Stones.

Alex James	British musician, songwriter, and cheese-maker, best known as the bassist of the band Blur. Part of the Fat Les collective.
Nick Kent	British rock critic, musician, and former contributor to *NME* and *The Face*.
Andrew Lloyd Webber	Popular West End and Broadway composer of musicals such as *Cats, Evita,* and *Phantom Of The Opera*.
Vivian MacKerrell	Actor and real-life inspiration for the Withnail character in *Withnail and I*.
Addi Merrill	Savage & Best PR from 1996 to 1999.
Dominic Mohan	British journalist and broadcaster who edited *The Sun*'s 'Bizarre' column between 1998 and 2003, before becoming *The Sun*'s editor in 2009.
Mike Muir	Lead vocalist for Californian thrash-metal band Suicidal Tendencies.
John Mulvey	*NME* features editor and writer during the 1990s, he moved on to edit *Uncut* and then *Mojo*.
Youssou N'Dour	Senegalese singer, songwriter, composer, and politician.
Kieran O'Brien	British television and film actor.
Barbara Orbison	German-born music producer/publisher. Manager and wife of Roy Orbison (d. December 6 2011).

Roy Orbison	American musician and singer famed for his dark, lovelorn ballads and emotional singing style (d. December 6 1988).
Marco Pirroni	British guitarist, songwriter, and record producer. Ex-guitarist with Adam & The Ants and possibly a member of The Wild Frontiers.
A.R. Rahman	Indian singer and soundtrack composer who sprang to international stardom in 2008 with his soundtrack to *Slumdog Millionaire*.
Lou Reed	American lead guitarist, songwriter, musician, and principal founder (together with John Cale) of The Velvet Underground (d. October 27 2013).
William Rice	Savage & Best PR (1995–99) who launched the music division of Purple PR in 2004.
Saffron	Singer, songwriter, actress, and lead singer of the electronica band Republica.
Tom Sheehan	Rock photographer who shot countless *Melody Maker* front covers in the 1990s. In recent years, Sheehan has published books of photography on Paul Weller, The Cure, Manic Street Preachers, and R.E.M.

Rav Singh   Showbiz editor of the *News Of The World* 2001–08.

Jo Skinny   One half of the stylist duo responsible for much of the look of the Britpop era.

Pat Skinny   The other half of the stylist duo responsible for much of the look of the Britpop era.

Mark E. Smith   Very British singer, songwriter, and musician who was the lead singer, lyricist, and sole constant member of The Fall (d. January 24 2018).

Dave Stewart   British musician, songwriter, and record producer, best known for Eurythmics, his successful partnership with Annie Lennox.

Joe Strummer   Co-founder, lyricist, rhythm guitarist, and lead vocalist of The Clash (d. December 22 2002).

Steve Sutherland   *Melody Maker* and *NME* editor during the 1990s.

Melissa Thompson   Former Best In Press employee and Savage & Best PR 1993–99.

Andrew 'Tiny' Wood   Often called 'the most unlikely British rock star ever' and frontman for 90s prog-rock pioneers Ultrasound.

acknowledgements

With thanks to my agent Matthew Hamilton, Tom Seabrook and Nigel Osborne at Jawbone, everyone at Savage & Best—John Best, Melissa Thompson, Polly Birkbeck, Rachel Hendry, William Rice, Addi Merrill, Sue Whitehouse, Debbie Rawlings—Grace Holbrook, Saul Galpern, Mel Bell, Samantha Preston, Sophie Williams, Sian Davies, Jonathan Carricker, Scout Savidge for the cover concept, and Michael Halpin for his Britpop timeline.

ALSO AVAILABLE IN PRINT AND EBOOK EDITIONS FROM JAWBONE PRESS